ELISE

ELISE

REBIRTH OF THE TRUE LOTUS

R295 LTF

Alastair Clements

Foreword by Adrian Newey

To Dad
Rediscover the car nut within and buy another Lotus.

© Alastair Clements 2003

First published in 2003

A catalogue record for this book is available from the British Library

ISBN 1 85960 857 4

Library of Congress catalog card no. 2002117292

Published by Haynes Publishing, Sparkford,
Yeovil, Somerset, BA22 7JJ, UK

Tel: 01963 442030 Fax: 01963 440001
Int. tel: +44 1963 442030 Int. fax: +44 1963 440001
E-mail: sales@haynes-manuals.co.uk
Website: www.haynes.co.uk

Haynes North America, Inc.,
861 Lawrence Drive, Newbury Park,
California 91320, USA

Printed and bound in England by J. H. Haynes & Co. Ltd, Sparkford

Contents

Foreword
by Adrian Newey
Technical Director, McLaren International Ltd

I'm not sure at exactly what age I decided that the career path I would most like to pursue would be that of designing racing cars, but it was quite early. A significant contribution to this passion was the family purchase in 1968, when I was nine, of a Lotus Elan S4 kit. I watched my Father with avid interest as he built the kit over the following weeks, and as a boy I loved going to and from school in that car, even learning to drive in it when I was 11 years old. My Father also became hooked on Elans, performing all his own servicing, and adding to the S4 as we became an all Elan family with the purchase of a second-hand Elan +2 in 1970 and an Elan Sprint kit in 1971.

The Sprint was heavily tuned over the following years, with a 170-horsepower Vegantune engine and ZF gearbox. My Father gave me the Sprint when I was 24, and between us we did about 170,000 miles in that car, always as our primary means of transport, with all the maintenance that entailed!

The value of a small, light, efficient and fine handling sports car of sufficient practicality to be used everyday, was thus engraved into my childhood. Unfortunately, through the eighties and early nineties it appeared to be a value lost on car manufacturers the world over including, shame of shame, Lotus.

In 1995 that finally changed – a manufacturer started building such a car again and, best of all, it was Lotus. The Elise is in every way a successor to the Elan ethos and one which, despite the huge social and environmental changes between the sixties and today, is still every bit as in keeping with the Lotus tradition, and just as desirable.

Technically, with the Elise chassis construction method of bonded aluminium extrusions and un-stressed fibreglass body, Lotus has made a step that is just as innovative as Chapman's Elan backbone chassis and semi-stressed fibreglass body. The extension of the extrusion method into production of parts such as the pedals and suspension uprights produces a car that has a homogenous 'designed by one person' feel that is generally lost in today's bland corporate products. Overall, the Elise is a car that you can appreciate, be it as an engineer, enthusiast or schoolboy, whether you are looking at it (even if the styling is not to everybody's taste) or driving it.

And my Elise? Well I have also inherited my Father's desire to modify the base product, so mine has grown a turbocharger along with various other modifications to tailor it more exactly to what I wanted.

Like the Elan, the simple design of the Elise lends itself to modification, whether by the factory or by an individual. It is a car to enjoy both through ownership and driving. This book provides a fascinating insight to how the Elise came to be and how it has been developed since.

Adrian Newey at the wheel of his modified Elise. (Paul Harmer/CCC)

Introduction: The sports car returns

Open any motoring magazine published since September 1995 and you won't have to look too hard to find reams of hyperbole extolling the virtues of a little car called Elise: the saviour of Lotus, the rebirth of the true sports car. This quirky little stripped-out skateboard is a real racer for the road, yet displays the impeccable manners and perfect compromise between comfortable ride and superb handling for which Lotus cars have become legendary. And it is a true Lotus; a return to the classic principles of innovation and performance through light weight, as pioneered by the company's founder and inspiration, Colin Chapman.

In the early 1990s Lotus was lost. Pursuit of the supercar landed the firm in a wilderness a world away from its beginnings as a builder of pared down, innovative, pure driving machines. Even the sharp-suited, Peter Stevens-penned front-drive Elan could not haul the Lotus name away from an association with flogging dead horses such as the Excel, which began as the Elite of 1974 yet survived until 1992, or the 20-year-old Esprit. Ironically, the car that was to turn those fortunes around and give the Norfolk firm a new direction and a measure of stability – at least temporarily – was not a supercar at all, but one that returned to its roots. The car that would steal the headlines and return the Lotus name to the A-list of sports car manufacturers was one that was born of simplicity through engineering innovation. Pure Lotus.

And the Elise would appear, despite the upheavals that went on around it. Ownership of Group Lotus would shift across the seas to Malaysia, yet the Elise would not be diverted from its mission to remind the European buying public – and maybe one day America

– why we love the motor car so much. The timing of its launch at the 1995 Frankfurt Motor Show was perfect, riding on a wave of Lotus fever thanks to projects such as the new and improved Elan S2 and the Type 108 Lotus Sport Bicycle which carried Chris Boardman to gold in the 4,000 metres race at the 1992 Barcelona Olympic Games.

The turn of the 1990s saw a renaissance for open-top enthusiasts on a budget, as a rash of affordable sports cars appeared, but most were little more than hatchbacks in drag. The success of the Elise showed the wealth of drivers that had been waiting for

A classic marque returns to form – a Lotus Elise nose badge. (Tony Baker)

such a car, and the breath of fresh air it brought to the marketplace quickly became a hurricane, blowing softer sportsters such as the MGF, Mazda MX5 and BMW Z3 into the weeds. It introduced a new generation to the kind of driver appeal that fans of the legendary Seven, Elan and Europa had long raved about, adding vivid performance and modern-day reliability. For owners, it was more than just a means of transport, generating real enthusiasts and even tempting classic car fans away from oily rags and socket sets to return to the dreaded modern motorcar.

It was even applauded by the discerning and obsessive Lotus followers, who recognised it for what it is, a car that in terms of technology and innovation created the kind of revolutionary ripple through the motor industry not seen since the marque introduced its glassfibre monocoque Elite, nearly 40 years before. Where the M100 Elan was sometimes criticised as being bland, the Elise is anything but. Whether it is desire or hatred, its wacky styling always prompts extremes of opinion and, considering the fact that in 2002 it became the best-selling Lotus model of all time, the Elise's cheeky shape is obviously much more admired than scorned.

While demand for the car continued to grow, prompting the Hethel marque to turn it from a limited-volume experiment into a full production car, Lotus never rested on its laurels. The Elise was constantly developed, making it faster, grippier and even more competent on and off track. Hot-rod versions followed as the engine was progressively developed to spawn the ultimate roadgoing Elises: the breathtaking Exige and the truly barking 340R. In 2000 came an all-new Elise with aggressive new looks, even more grip and more refinement for the increasing number of buyers using their cars every day.

With the familiarity of the Elise today, it is hard to imagine that, had its development gone down a different path, we could have ended up with a front-engined, gullwing-doored, Rover-badged, step-in Elise. But as history reveals, circumstance, serendipity and perseverance with an untested yet truly innovative concept conspired to bring inspiration to Lotus, and a real treat to car enthusiasts.

Acknowledgements

Grateful thanks to Haynes Publishing and especially to Mark Hughes for his endless patience – and for asking me to do this. To James Elliott for his help and advice throughout, and to Richard Heseltine and Paul Breckenridge for their selfless offer to drive Elises for Tony Baker's excellent photography. Also to Philippa Woodcock and technical guru Matt Jennings.

Thanks to all at Group Lotus: Chris Arnold, Matt Becker, Russell Carr, Steve Crijns, Morris Dowton, Alastair Florance, Gavan Kershaw, Keith Hare, Dawn Manwaring, Alastair McQueen, Richard Rackham, Ken Sears, Anthony Shute, and to former Lotus man Julian Thomson.

Finally, thanks to Clive Chapman at Classic Team Lotus, Rob Aherne at *Autocar*, Stuart Harris at Vauxhall, Luke Plummer at Ducati UK, and to John Shorrocks, Chris Monk and particularly Bobby Bell at Bell & Colvill.

In its element – a Lotus Elise on the open road. (Tony Baker)

1 **From concept**
to crowd-puller

The story of the Elise begins in August 1993 with the acquisition of Group Lotus by the Italian firm Bugatti Industries, headed by the dynamic Romano Artioli. With new owners came an impetus to create while also returning to the Lotus core values, namely innovative, superb handling performance cars that achieve their speed by light weight rather than huge power.

After the comparative failure of the M100 Elan, Tony Shute was put in charge of the project, codenamed M111, to realise a car that would revive the ideals of company founder Colin Chapman. The M111 was one of a range of vehicles, including a V8 2+2, driven by Artioli's passion to revive the marque, but it was the only car to make it to the road. Although a modern interpretation of the minimalist Lotus Seven had been mooted as early as April 1992, it had been a front-engined concept with a transaxle in the rear. Tagged 'Step-in car', the project began with a 575kg (1,268lb) target weight to offer excellent performance and fuel efficiency from a smaller engine to make it more environmentally friendly.

To fund the project, cash-strapped Lotus Cars had to call on big brother Lotus Engineering, liberating its research budget for two years. In return, the M111 had to be a technical *tour de force*, an advertisement for the abilities of this world-renowned consultancy. Given the board's blessing in January 1994, it was conceived as a pure toy, with a total of around 2,700 cars to be built in a three-year run, allowing the designers to go wild with an utterly uncompromised machine. But in addition to tight budgets

there were tight time constraints, the car required to be turned from concept to production-ready vehicle in two years, to take over from the Elan S2. 'We had the production line working to make those cars, but once it stopped we had nothing to go down that line,' said Tony Shute, 'that was the need for the rapid introduction of the Elise programme.'

In addition to exploiting the funds and facilities of Lotus Engineering, Lotus Cars also teamed up with the Rover Group, as Shute explained: 'They were very interested in aluminium structures, so it was set up as a joint project. We would put a car into production, they would learn about aluminium structures and in return we would be able to use bits out of their parts bin.' Unfortunately, the partnership was scuppered by the 1994 sale of Rover by owner British Aerospace, but by then Lotus was well along the path that would lead to the Elise. 'BMW came along and bought out Rover,' continued Shute, 'at the time Rover said: "We can't really carry on because we're going to have to regroup, but you carry on and we'll be happy to supply you with parts".' But it was a big risk for a small company, particularly one with such a precarious financial history, to go it alone, as Shute recalled: 'Any car is going to become make or break; they are always a very significant investment. Even though the background of Lotus was this type of car, it was a new market for us, so that was a bit of a risk.'

The close-knit project team of designers, engineers and technicians began to hammer out what they wanted for M111, the consensus being that it had to be open and rear-wheel-drive, and had to avoid the cost and complexity of the M100. The team wanted the thrills and simplicity of a Lotus Seven and the combination of looks, comfort and driving pleasure of the classic Type 26 Elan. Having looked at front-engine, front-drive and front-engine, rear-drive, the team opted for the thoroughly modern mid-engined approach. 'It was relatively low in terms of retail cost for us,' Shute explained, 'to achieve that you've got to use a high-volume engine and gearbox. The only areas they come from are front-wheel-drive cars because they are the ones built in volume. You can either take a unit like that and stick it in the front – we'd done that with the Elan – or stick it in the back. It's much easier to achieve decelerations in the front end of the car, which is what most crash legislation was about then, if you've got nothing in the way. If you've got an empty void you can manage the energy dissipation, if you've got a solid lump of engine, particularly with a short car, it becomes quite tricky.'

To remind themselves what a light car consisted of, Lotus technicians bought, weighed and assembled a Caterham Seven kit, but both designers and engineers decided the new car would be a very different beast. The Seven dates back to 1957 and it was important not to copy the cycle-winged wild child, but rather to create a truly modern interpretation that was equally thrilling. Head of design Julian Thomson and his team were already champing at the bit when approached by Bugatti director Giampaulo Benedini to be given a long-awaited chance to create a new Lotus. 'It was a rather blank-sheet car,' explained Thomson, 'if you look at Lotus design philosophy through the years and try to find a lineage there really isn't one. We'd done some pretty uneven production cars and we wanted to say what Lotus was all about, it had to really look like a Lotus.' Blank sheet it may have been, but that sheet was soon filled with inspiration from the past, not to mention the minimalist beauty and no-compromise attitude of the Ducati 916 superbike.

The Julian Thomson sketch chosen as the preferred design for Project M111. (Lotus)

A Lotus Seven, Elan, 23, Elan M100 and a Ferrari Dino were brought into the studio to inspire the design team. (Lotus)

Former head of Lotus Design, Julian Thomson with his much-loved Ferrari Dino, one of the all-time great mid-engined sports cars. (Keith Eden)

Early in the process, Lotus Design gathered a Lotus 23 racer, Lotus/Caterham Seven and both first- and second-generation Elans, the 1960s car belonging to Tony Shute's wife. There was also Julian Thomson's own Ferrari Dino, one of the finest mid-engined road cars of all time. But it was to be the Lotus 23 that really captured the designers' imagination, particularly as it was a car that Benedini owned, and it provided a prototype for simplicity, performance through light weight and a recognisable Lotus face. The giant-killing Type 23 sports racer first appeared in 1962 with Cosworth-Ford power, but as the 23B it became the first car to feature the superb Lotus-Ford twin-cam engine. It stood for exceptional speed without being intimidating, retaining a delicacy lost in the brutal V8-powered Lotus 30 and 40 sports racers.

'It is retro, unashamedly so,' said Thomson of his design. 'Inspiration really came from cars of the '60s and '70s; I'm really fond of the Targa Florio racing cars of that era. Certainly the original racing

[Ferrari] Dino 206SP was quite an inspiration, the 23 was, but also certain cars that were a bit more modern but had beautiful proportions like the [Ford] GT40 and the [Lamborghini] Miura.' The final car's purposeful stance was very reminiscent

The delicate Type 23 sports-racer of the 1960s provided many cues for the M111. (LAT)

An early Russell Carr sketch for the 'Step-in car' shows influence from the Lotus Seven. (Lotus)

The revolutionary glassfibre monocoque Type 14 Lotus Elite of 1957 was beautiful, but so costly to make that it nearly bankrupted the firm. (LAT)

appropriate to revive cues from the Europa, which was the first mid-engined Lotus production car when it was launched in 1966. Like the M111, it used a front-wheel-drive hatchback engine, from the Renault 16, and became legendary for its sensational handling and roadholding. The M111's 'Lotus face' features a grille aperture that apes that of the Europa and the tiny and beautiful Type 26 Elan of 1962, often cited as the firm's finest road car. Although intended to capture the spirit of the past without being a pastiche, the brief did restrict the team's freedom and has been accused of being too derivative. But Thomson defends the decision: 'If you were to do it now you probably wouldn't play on the retro thing quite as much, but only because people have an idea of what Lotus stands for; we re-established that and gave ourselves the opportunity to move on from there. I think it was the right thing to do at the time. Retro was very controversial, but since the Elise came out we've had things like the Beetle production car, the Prowler, the new MINI, we were before all of those. One thing that is perhaps a little confusing is

of a sports racer, and details such as the central twin tailpipes with flanking vents scream GT40. Look hard at the Elise and you start to see further precedent from Lotus's past. The front light treatment is pure Europa, a nod to the classic John Frayling-penned Type 46 with its indicators moved up and in to the bonnet to increase visibility on such a low car. It seems

Colin Chapman, founder and inspiration for the engineers at Group Lotus, with an early example of the 'wedge' Esprit supercar. (LAT)

Lotus:
potted
history of
a timeless
marque

The story of Lotus began in 1928 in Richmond, Surrey with the birth of Anthony Colin Bruce Chapman, initials familiar to owners of Lotus-badged cars. Trained as an engineer, Chapman served with the RAF before motoring became a career, when he began dealing in used cars. In 1947, he created the first Lotus, a special based on a tired 1920 Austin Seven saloon, which he trialled with some success. Chapman expanded his ideas with brothers and fellow 750 Motor Club members Michael and Nigel Allen, the more accomplished Ford sidevalve-powered MkII arriving in 1959. But it wasn't until the spindly MkIII that customers could buy their own examples of the fledgling marque. On 1 January 1952, the Lotus Engineering Company was formed in partnership with Michael, although he was to leave before the year was out after the first of numerous financial scares hit the firm. The first 'production' Lotus, the MkVI, followed a year later and featured stressed aluminium panels riveted to a tubular spaceframe chassis.

Chapman had left his job in 1954 to concentrate on building cars, the stable behind his father's pub in Hornsey, North London serving as a makeshift factory. The firm became known as Lotus Cars Ltd from 1955 and just two years later it launched a duo of superb road cars at the Earls Court Motor Show. The spartan road-racer Seven was to become a legend as the ultimate in driver appeal and the revolutionary glassfibre monocoque Type 14 Elite, although beautiful, was so expensive to make that it nearly killed the firm.

Building an enviable reputation for exceptional sports-racers such as the MkIX, Eleven, and Type 15, Lotus Cars opened its first proper factory in Cheshunt, Hertfordshire, in 1959. Lotus Components Ltd was formed to look after customer racing cars and Seven production. Chapman's innovation began to pay real dividends with his monocoque 25 in 1962, which with Graham Hill, brought Team Lotus the first of five Grand Prix drivers' world championship titles. Chapman was an accomplished racer himself, his talents behind the wheel contributing to his strong relationships with drivers, particularly Jim Clark and Mario Andretti.

'Chunky', so-called for dimensions that ensured Lotus cars were a perfect fit for 5ft 8in drivers, next turned his attention to transforming the lowly Ford Consul Cortina saloon into a race and rally legend. Adding the superb Lotus twin-cam head (developed for the 23 and Elan in 1962) to Ford's engine brought the Lotus-Cortina in 1963. It was the first of many unorthodox collaborations, which later sired Sunbeam-Lotus, Lotus-Carlton and Lotus-Proton, whose engine and suspension tweaks turned stodgy motors into proficient performers.

Expansion required another move in 1966 to a former US Air Force base in Hethel, Norfolk, the new site offering more space and a test track on which to hone those famous chassis. The Lotus Group, consisting of Lotus Cars Ltd, Lotus Components Ltd and Team Lotus Ltd, was floated as a public company in 1969, Chapman serving not only as head of Lotus Cars, but also team manager for the successful Team Lotus Grand Prix team.

With the supercar Esprit being readied for its 1975 Paris Salon unveiling, the fuel crisis hit and the firm nearly went bust, the workforce dropping from 830 to 385. But this was just one of many storms weathered by a firm always walking a financial tightrope. In 1977, American Express gave Lotus a credit line, the lucrative DeLorean project bringing further security a year on, one of many projects to come under the Lotus Engineering consultancy banner in 1980. A technical cooperation deal with Toyota was announced by Chapman in 1981, but in addition to laying the groundwork for the MR2 (Mid-engine, Rear-drive, 2-seater) the deal led to Toyota buying 15 per cent of the firm and providing a cheap source of components for Lotus products. Times became turbulent for the firm after Chapman's death at the age of just 54 on 16 December 1982, and without his driving force it drifted away from the peak of top level competition.

After making a loss in 1981, the American market all but disappeared the following year, and in 1983, British Car Auctions and Toyota become major shareholders. Financial difficulties continued to build, culminating in General Motors acquiring a large share of Group Lotus plc in 1986. By now, Lotus was becoming a hot potato and in 1993 it passed to Bugatti Industries, following the success of the Type 108 pursuit bike that took Chris Boardman to Olympic Gold in Barcelona 1992.

The year 1995 was one of mixed fortunes, as the Elise was unveiled at the Frankfurt show, bringing renewed ambition, but Lotus quit Formula One and parent company Bugatti went into receivership. In 1996, Malaysian concern Proton acquired a controlling share in Group Lotus, finally providing the financial backing to make a success of the Elise.

that the car has so much new technology inside, but it's clothed in a heritage body.'

'Step-in car' was conceived almost as a four-wheeled motorbike, avoiding the need for the additional weight and development costs of a roof and doors, not to mention the associated paraphernalia such as locks and windows. But a doorless car was inherently compromised, and the designers' hopes of creating removable gullwing doors were vetoed by the body engineering department as too complex, too costly and too

Regulations requiring cut-down sills and an external step gave the 'Step-in car' a beach-buggy look and forced Lotus to consider adding doors; a sketch by Russell Carr. (Lotus)

time-consuming to resolve. The decision was made for them when the legal department pointed out that the regulations for step-over height would require a 30mm step or drop in height for the sills, which would ruin the lines of car, making it look too much like a beach buggy. 'We soon realised that we can't really sell any vehicles in northern Europe which don't have some degree of weather-proof equipment,' said Tony Shute. 'So it had to have a roof and suddenly you have all this complexity. Essentially cars have doors on them for very good reasons; it gives you an extra degree of refinement.'

The design evolves

In February 1994, with the project just months old, Bugatti dropped a bombshell on Lotus Design by revealing it had also asked a number of external stylists to prepare proposals for the M111. Among 11 illustrious design houses and individuals to offer their services were Tom Tjaarda, Peter Stevens, IDEA and Zagato, so the team was

understandably concerned as it was very much make-or-break time for the design consultancy. 'Artioli had a pretty good relationship with the key Italian styling houses through setting up Bugatti and they all wanted a piece of the action,' said Thomson, 'they wanted publicity and also the body engineering work later on. In the event we had a review and were told to stick this stuff up in the studio. We were so ahead not only in our design, we had scale models of it at that point, but also we had a chassis buck made up out of wood on the floor.' When the Lotus board arrived to choose a design, the conventional alternatives paled alongside the forward-thinking in-house proposal and to the team's great relief it was chosen.

To go from sketched ideas to a final design, Lotus used a traditional approach. Starting with a full-size buck, the stylists worked with pens, paper and clay rather than the mouse and computer screen of today. There were computer-aided design (CAD) models made of the styling and structure, but only after most problems had been resolved in full-size drawings, created with removable tape to enable alterations to be made easily. Running alongside this process were the one third-scale models, fashioned in clay then moulded in glassfibre. The first of these was completed at the close of 1993, but it was Julian Thomson's model of March the following year that was chosen as the way forward and scanned into a computer to give the dimensions for the full-size clay. It was machined in May from a layer of clay over a timber and polystyrene base, modellers refining the shape to provide a prototype for the final body style. As

inputs came in from styling, engineering and production departments, stylist Andrew Hill was on hand to mediate and make sure the original design intentions would not be compromised on the way to production. 'There was the occasional conflict,' recalled Thomson, 'but it did run pretty smoothly for a project like that and there was a core team of about five to ten key people that really understood it. On nitty-gritty design issues near the end of the project the Italians, who are heavily design-orientated, always came down on our side.'

A problem did arise however when a third-scale model of the proposed design was

Lotus 23 inspiration is clear in this Russell Carr sketch for the 'Step-in car' with a gullwing style roof. (Lotus)

A T-bar roof was one of the options considered to ensure the M111 remained as stiff as possible despite the open roof; a sketch by Julian Thomson. (Lotus)

Bugatti boss Romano Artioli invited a selection of stylists to prepare competing proposals for the new Lotus; this rendering is by Tom Tjaarda. (Tom Tjaarda)

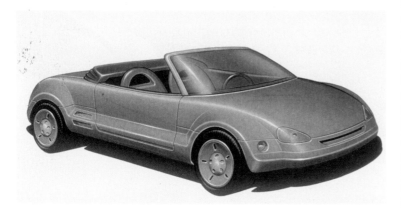

taken to the Motor Industry Research Association (MIRA) wind tunnel. With the car being very styling-led, and with top speed less important than acceleration and handling, aerodynamics had taken something of a back seat. Aerodynamicist Richard Hill found that the front intake with bonnet exit offered good downforce on the nose, and the flat floor with NACA-ducted undertray beneath the engine formed a racing car-style underbody diffuser. But the clean Lotus 23-style rounded rump generated rear-end lift, not ideal for a lightweight rear-drive sports car. To combat the effect, Hill jury-rigged clay aerodynamic aids on the model, adding a rear wing, raising the rear flying buttresses and further enclosing the wheelarches. Although some of the add-ons were fussy, the spoiler in particular looking like a knife left stuck in the butter, they did at the same time add aggression. 'It was a bit of an unknown,' said Thomson, who was not keen on altering his design at such a late stage. 'It was a very light mid-engined car so we were on the cautious side in terms of lift-off oversteer and I think they were probably right. But, being Lotus, the information came too late and by then we had committed to a lot of the

surfaces of the car so it had to be a stuck-on piece. The original model was much nicer, I don't particularly like the spoiler on the back.' Another dispute to tax Thomson's patience was with the body engineers, who wanted larger body moulds to allow for shrinkage: 'The car didn't need those huge wheelarches, especially at the back. That was our body engineering department being overly cautious about the amount the body would shrink. The car just got bigger and bigger and when they did make it, it didn't shrink so the wheels are too inset at the back of the car.'

Interior and exterior surfaces were designed in tandem, the cabin in particular requiring close contact with the chassis engineers as the structure remained almost entirely exposed, acting both as a styling detail and a major saving in cost and weight. The low-slung driving position and near-

perfect arrangement of windscreen, seats, wheel and pedals were decided right at the start in a wood and cardboard buck on the studio floor, which also modelled the sense of security of having the chassis wrapped around you. The interior's intimacy was once again a nod to the past, as Thomson explained. 'We wanted the first generation Elan compactness in the cockpit; that pure driving machine sensation.' Tony Shute's passion for light weight really shows itself, with no carpets, no stereo and wipe-clean surfaces a legacy of the roofless 'Step-in car' concept.

Style meets structure

One of the greatest qualities of the M111 is its seamless combination of styling and structure. This blend of engineering and design is, for the most part, thanks to the close friendship of head of design Julian

Designers used a cardboard and timber buck to resolve the new car's driving position and internal proportions. (Lotus)

The rear view of Julian Thomson's chosen scale model. (Author)

Stylist Russell Carr resolves detail design changes on the full-size tape drawing. (Lotus)

Thomson and lead chassis engineer Richard Rackham, each serving as Best Man at the other's wedding. Their strong empathy meant the project avoided the time-consuming conflict that often occurs between the two disciplines. 'We were both single at the time,' recalled Rackham, 'we were able to focus totally, it really took over our lives for a couple of years.' It also helped that the forward-thinking Rackham avoided the blinkered, conventional view of many engineers, boasting a desire to create elegant solutions to complicated problems. 'He's a very exceptional engineer because he can appreciate the art of beautiful engineering,' said Thomson, 'it's very rare to find and I guess Colin Chapman and William Lyons, all the greats, were like that. Look at their work and they're not necessarily designed aesthetically, but by their very purity they look fantastic.'

Chassis innovation is nothing new at Lotus, witness the novel approaches of the ultra-light MkVI spaceframe, the glassfibre monocoque Elite or the 'floating rafts' of the M100 Elan. The M111 followed this tradition, Rackham fighting off more conventional proposals both from in-house

and from the Peter Stevens concern to achieve his forward-thinking structure. 'I don't think pure design is a conscious process,' he modestly suggested, 'you gather all the limitations and requirements and the solution evolves. Some people like to design using tried and tested materials and principles; I think Chapman was one of those people looking for stuff that people hadn't done before. I'm most interested in what's going to come, not what's been.'

Ever since the 1962 Elan, Lotus had been building cars with a light backbone chassis,

Modellers work on the full-size M111 clay model in the design studio. (Lotus)

The completed full-size clay model part-covered with highlighting film to show how its surfaces reflected the light. (Lotus)

Modellers working on the near-complete interior clay. (Lotus)

but modern crash regulations are difficult to meet without adding excessive weight when the structure runs down the centre of the car. Rackham decided to run the structure around the outside of the cockpit so it could double-up as crash protection. The difficulty then arises in the size of the chassis, and with lightness the watchword for the project, it seemed obvious it would be made either of aluminium or composites. With costs of the latter being prohibitively high, the task became one of making an aluminium structure sufficiently innovative to be an advertisement for the abilities of Lotus Engineering. Early work with Rover Group set Rackham along the path, as he explained: 'They were looking to use extrusions in the design of a vehicle. So the task was to design a car using extrusions, not to think of a new way. Then BMW bought Rover, but we realised by then the advantages of this

extruded system.' The extrusion process had previously been used in the building industry, for items such as greenhouses and window frames, and involves heating aluminium until it goes soft then ramming it through a die to give a long member of constant section.

Another product of the partnership with Rover had been an introduction to Hydro Aluminium, part of Norsk Hydro, which became a collaborative partner to provide the production capability for the chassis. Hydro's main business was extruded tonnage of aluminium for the construction industry, but it had recently set up an automotive structures department in an effort to break into the motoring world. 'There was an opportunity to work with Lotus,' said Tony Shute, 'and although the car is irrelevant in terms of volume, it is real and does go down a production line and does meet European vehicle type approval. So by working with us

they could prove that they have the know-how and technology to do projects of this type.' Rackham explained the advantages of an extruded structure: 'You can put interlocks and fixings for other parts of the car into the extrusion without any extra cost, the extrusion die costs a few thousand pounds whether it's a rectangle or a complex shape.' Because the process is so quick and simple, Lotus paid for the weight of material rather than individual parts, but it wasn't all easy: 'There is no previous work to base the design upon,' Rackham continued. 'So to begin with it was very frustrating because you can't treat aluminium like steel, it's an entirely different material.' One thing that is expensive to do with extrusions is bend them, so at first Rackham avoided curves in the design, resorting to cutting and reforming the chassis aft of the cabin on prototypes to provide engine mounts. But for

the final car he worked with Hydro in pursuit of an elegant arc that required the main side members being sent to Raufoss Automotive in the UK, which also manufactured some of the smaller extrusions, to be stretch-bent before returning to Denmark for assembly.

Once he had got into what he referred to as an 'extrusions mindset', Rackham realised that he could design cheap and elegant replacements for standard parts throughout the car. So it was that the Elise became the first car to feature extruded aluminium suspension uprights, in addition to an extruded steering column bracket. When the brief changed to include doors, simple extrusions provided both a method for hanging the door and further side-impact protection, but it was trying to fit a Metro pedal box that prompted Rackham's masterpiece. 'Pedal box assemblies from

Close friends Richard Rackham and Julian Thomson served as Best Man at each other's weddings. (Julian Thomson)

Learning
from its
mistakes:
the 'new'
Elan

The M100 Elan had every right to be a success. *Autocar and Motor* hailed it 'the most significant British sports car to appear for 25 years.' *Car* went further with 'one of the most significant sports cars ever launched – and one of the most desirable.' A true Lotus great then? Yes and no. The Elan was certainly a technical *tour de force*, Hethel's first attempt at driving the 'wrong' wheels is often cited as the greatest front-drive chassis of all time. Unfortunately, many felt that it lacked soul, something the Elise has in spades.

Styled by Peter Stevens, the M100 ushered in a new era at Lotus after decades of the aggressive 'wedge' look and followed Stevens's successful 1987 update of the Esprit. The short-wheelbase Elan had a squat stance, with a stubby nose and a chubby tail, but was well received by both press and public when launched at the 1989 London Motorfair. Under the composite body panels were unconventional mechanicals. There was the classic steel backbone chassis, but up front it boasted a novel alloy floating raft 'interactive wishbone' system, giving the compliance to absorb bumps yet maintaining the front wheels' geometry in the twisty bits. The power unit was a 130bhp, 16-valve 1,588cc Isuzu twin-cam 'four', which shifted the 1,032kg (2,276lb) car along fairly well. But it really came alive with the turbocharged 165bhp SE, a

flying machine that reached 60mph (96.5km/h) from rest in 6.7 seconds and offered 137mph (219km/h) flat out. With its five-speed transaxle it was also a refined long-distance car and the clever suspension gave the traditionally superb Lotus ride quality. Inside, it was far from inspiring, with a plasticky dashboard more suited to a boring hatchback, perhaps befitting a machine conceived as the car VW Golf GTi owners would aspire to. But the seats were good, the driving position excellent, and there was a decent boot and such luxuries as central locking, power steering and electric windows and mirrors to make it a usable daily driver.

The fact that the front wheels were being driven divorced the design from its predecessors, but the driving experience was pure Lotus. There was none of the usual torque steer or understeer of a front-drive car, and the neutral chassis made it easy to drive quickly and it was a demon cross country. But perhaps it was too easy, too comfortable, lacking the raw appeal of a Lotus. 'I think where cars like the Elan may have fallen foul was that they were extremely competent, you get in and can drive quickly straight off,' said vehicle dynamics engineer Matt Becker. 'Point-to-point they were mind-blowingly fast and comfortable, the ride was excellent. But with something like an Elise you have to be a good driver to get the most from the car.'

The M100's complexity counted against it when it came to making a profit, as product manager Tony Shute explained: 'It was expensive to make and was designed for the US market, and that made the investment in terms of the programme very high. In reality the volumes weren't there for the US, but it was a very successful product in Europe.' Priced out of contention in the 'States by a

new luxury goods tax, the Elan relied heavily on European sales where the cheaper, rear-drive Mazda MX-5, which many saw as the true successor to the original Elan, provided stiff competition. The stringent quality standards of then-owner General Motors didn't help, and with the additional joy of a recession to contend with the costly Elan nearly ruined Lotus. GM canned the model in 1992, shortly before selling its stake in the firm, but less than two years after its death, the Elan was back as the new and improved S2, thanks to new owner Bugatti. 'We ended up with a stock of engines and gearboxes and the best way to realise those was to stick them into cars,' explained Shute, 'hence the S2 Elan.' There were numerous improvements to counteract criticism of the first car, with a new exhaust system giving a sportier note, an improved gearshift, revalved steering for improved feel and stiffer, more sporting suspension with larger wheels and tyres. Unfortunately, the new twin-cat exhaust sapped 10bhp, and extra weight contributed to considerably blunted performance, with 0–60mph now taking 7.3 seconds. But with paltry development costs and the tooling already prepared, the S2 was very profitable. Some 800 right-hand-drive Elan S2s were built, and with a total of less than 5,000 'new' Elans built it became an instant classic, with resale values remaining sky-high.

But that was not the end for the Elan, it still had a swansong to perform. In 1996, Lotus sold the rights and tooling to Kia, who inserted its normally aspirated 1.8-litre engine and sold it in the Asian market. Called the Kia Elan in South Korea, the model was not a great success in a marketplace where open cars traditionally struggle, but it soldiered on until 2000.

conventional pressed steel cars simply wouldn't fit the Elise's pure structure. But we realised that an extruded pedal box and pedals would fit beautifully, be very functional and very inexpensive. I would struggle to do anything better than that and it's one part I can claim was totally my own

work.' The pedal box consists of four extruded sections, with the pedal arms cut to thickness depending on the strength required.

Having resolved such a lightweight structure, the next stumbling block was how to join it together to ensure it remained stiff enough to offer superb handling. The team

The M100 Elan belied its front-drive underpinnings with superb neutral handling that enabled it to cover a twisty road quicker than many more powerful sports cars. (LAT)

After the first cars were criticised for their bland interior, Lotus tried to liven up the cabin of the Elan S2, but it still lacked the simple elegance of the Elise. (LAT)

abandoned the idea of welding the members together in favour of developing bonded joints, as used for many years in the aviation industry, but a first for a production car. 'To meet the weight targets you need very thin extrusions,' explained Shute, 'if you try welding it essentially damages them, so you need much thicker material. We took the bonded route as being in some ways lower risk because we knew the integrity of the joints would be really good. On the other side it was higher risk because nobody had done it in volume production before. All the effort went into developing a bonding system that was durable and affordable.'

A back-up chassis of the same shape was also designed using extrusions twice as thick to be welded together should a bonding system not materialise. Engineers Daryl Grieg and Kerry Osborne set to work in pursuit of a suitable method, working in association with Peter Bullivant-Clark at Hydro and CIBA Polymers in Cambridgeshire, which offered its high-strength and tough epoxy adhesive to withstand the combination of small area bonds and high impact resistance required for automotive applications. With no precedent available, Grieg and Osborne developed their own testing system, comparing welded, bonded and riveted overlapping joints and trying a variety of surface preparations for the aluminium itself. 'The key to the bonding is the pre-treatment

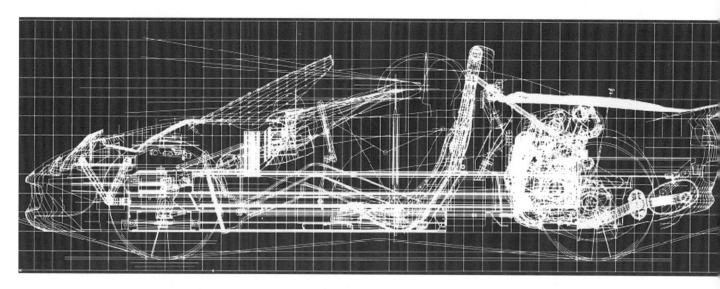

A computer-generated technical drawing shows the complete M111 package. (Lotus)

of aluminium,' Shute explained, 'anodising pre-oxidises it and makes it more stable.' The connections were tested to destruction by having weights dropped on them in a frame to simulate accidents, while others were sent away to be subjected to climatic conditions such as heat, cold and salt spray. The team realised it had succeeded when the aluminium failed long before the joint itself. Not only is a bonded joint much lighter than a weld, but it exploits the properties of the 6000-series aluminium employed in the M111 by forming a connection with a much larger area than a localised weld, so it can use all of the available strength. The Lotus bonding system holds international patents for its combination of anodised pre-treatment, bond and fasteners, with adhesive applied in a cross shape so that when the two members are pressed together the adhesive squeezes out to ensure full coverage.

One problem highlighted in the tests was that although bonded joints have high stress capacity, when they do fail they do so aggressively, if they suffer from peel at the edges of the bond. To counteract these problems, Grieg and Osborne came

up with a system of mechanical fasteners, which turned the assembled chassis into a semi-self-supporting structure so it can be sent to the oven to cure the adhesive. The

fastener selected was the German-made Ejot, a large-headed rivet used in the building industry and in the construction of commercial trailers. 'Peel prevention is really important in a crash, when metal starts to twist,' explained Rackham. 'The selection was based upon lots of mechanical testing and the Ejot fixings were far superior.'

Rackham's unconventional design is hard to categorise. Lotus calls it a spaceframe, and certainly it employs a hollow tubular perimeter frame with stiff torque tubes across the front and rear of the cabin connected by tubular box-section side members. But the tub-like bonded structure is a world away from the complex narrow gauge maze of tubing that the term conjures up, and it looks like a monocoque. Narrowest at the occupants' feet, the chassis widens out to the rear of the cabin, where an RAC-approved steel roll bar is attached and the side rails curl back to meet the rear subframe. These side members are multi-functional, serving as side-impact protection and ducting for the pipework and services that run fore and aft along the car. Attached to the chassis are front and rear 'clamshell' body sections, following Lotus precedent by being made from lightweight glassfibre. With few separate panels, removing body sections for servicing is simple and accident repair simply

26

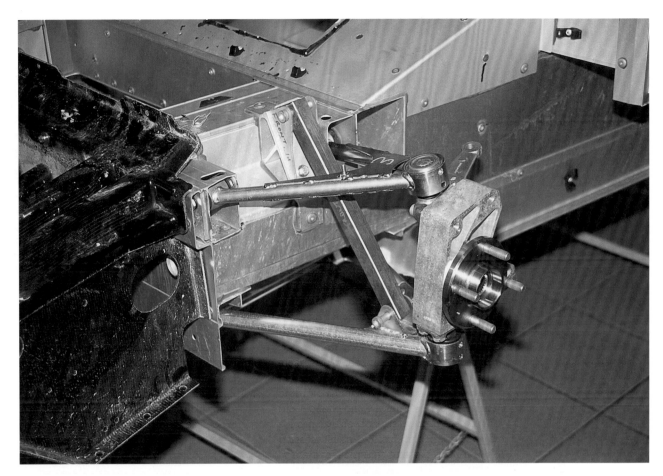

entails replacing the nose or tail. Not only is the chassis relatively cost-effective and simple to make, and suitable for either left- or right-hand drive, it also offers exceptional rigidity. Weighing in at a tiny 68kg (150lb), the chassis has a torsional stiffness of 10,133Nm per degree, rising to 11,000Nm per degree with the roll bar and body in place – incredible figures for an open car. 'I wouldn't say it's over-engineered,' concluded Rackham, 'but there's a huge safety factor in there and that's why there have been no failures in durability testing. I don't have any doubts about the bonding technique because very competent people developed the process.'

Another world first

As if the structure itself wasn't clever enough, Lotus achieved another first for a production car with the M111's moulded glassfibre crash structure, which was lighter and more efficient than traditional crumple zones. 'When you crush a piece of steel it crumples up and becomes a solid mass, usually about a seventh of the original length,' Rackham explained. 'When you crush a composite crash structure it turns to small particles and goes away so you can use the full crash length, which means the car can be shorter, which means lighter.' And true to form, the structure performs a variety of functions: supporting the radiator, the towing eye and the front clamshell, and ducting air into the radiator. In case of an accident, the car just needs a replacement part bonded on to the front of the chassis. As Tony Shute explained, the crash structure was developed separately to the chassis: 'Because of the

The M111 was the first production car to use lightweight aluminium extruded suspension uprights, designed by Richard Rackham. (Author)

Richard Rackham solved the complex issue of fitting a pedal box and pedals by designing a functional yet elegant set of extrusions. (Lotus)

modular nature of the car we could work in parallel so all the crash work was done using a steel girder frame, which we dumped into the wall at Millbrook [Proving Ground]. That could be developed off-line and when the chassis came along we married the two together.'

From the moment the decision was taken to make the M111 a mid-engined car, the

search was on for a suitable power unit. The 16-valve Renault Clio motor was considered, but its weight, and the relationship formed with Rover in the early stages of the project, persuaded Lotus to look to the Longbridge firm. Fortunately, they made the ideal engine, the light, compact and dynamic K-series 'four', first seen in the Rover 200 of 1989. Originally conceived as a 1.4 in

1984, the all-alloy, belt-driven twin-cam 16-valve K16 was enlarged with a longer stroke to 1,796cc for the MGF, launched at Geneva in 1995. The engine met Lotus's criteria for cost and weight perfectly, at just 130kg (287lb) with its transmission, and, once confident that the two models would not clash, Rover agreed to supply the unit in its basic (118bhp) form. It was appropriately innovative for a Lotus, featuring a clever construction of layers of aluminium alloy held together by ten 16in through-bolts, adding strength by keeping the structure in constant compression. It also employed self-adjusting hydraulic tappets and Bosch multi-point fuel injection controlled by a modular engine management system (MEMS).

With the M111 being so light, the low power output was more than enough to put the performance of the new Lotus a league ahead of the MG, while also capitalising on the small and unstressed unit's reputation for reliability and economy. The largely unaltered K-series, with five-speed manual transaxle, was slotted into the chassis transversely, unlike the longitudinal location of the Europa, to avoid making the car too long and compromising interior space. But the layout had its drawbacks, shifting the weight distribution to 60 per cent over the rear. 'If you use a transverse mid-engine layout you can't move the mass further forward from the rear wheels,' explained Lotus evaluation engineer Alastair McQueen, 'if you have a longitudinal layout like the Esprit you can move the engine mass a bit further forward.'

As 1994 drew to a close, Hydro delivered the first completed chassis and a team of

Richard Rackham's extruded and bonded aluminium chassis is not only light and revolutionary, but beautiful too. Chromed wishbones and aluminium rear subframe were for display purposes only. (Lotus)

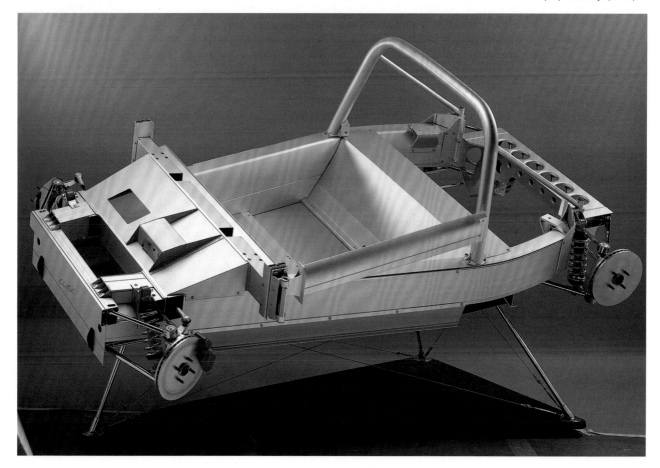

engineers descended on it to try to get an M111 running before the company closed for the winter break. Just four weeks later, on a freezing Christmas Eve, Prototype 1 headed on to the Hethel test track under its own power. It may have been bodyless, with just a screen and a pair of stuck-on headlights, but Tony Shute recalled that the potential was clear. 'The car straight out of the box was really good and the comfort was amazing.' The ride and handling engineers seemed equally blown away by the prototype's performance. 'You could instantly see the direction the car was going,' said Gavan Kershaw. 'It had razor-sharp response, the seating position was right, as were the height off the ground and the steering wheel position. No-one had gone down that route, so no-one could really see the benefits of it until you drove it. I remember being taken out by Tony [Shute] in the very first car and thinking "this has moved the plot on and this is just a development car" – the potential was massive.'

That first night run on an icy Hethel track was cut short as a heater pipe came loose and covered Shute with coolant. But in the New Year, Prototype 1 grew a hood and dummy wings from a Caterham Seven before being sent off to begin durability testing at Millbrook proving ground. After 1,000 miles of pounding around the cobbles of the Belgian Pavé test, the bonded chassis was proving its worth, showing no failures in conditions where a welded frame may well have suffered. However, it was the end of the line for the aluminium rear subframe. 'That particular part of the structure has many bolted joints,' explained Rackham, 'the subframe has to bolt to the tub, the rear suspension bolts to the subframe and the exhaust hangs off the back. When you try to resolve those loads in the directions of the extrusions it all gets rather complex, it just doesn't want to be made from aluminium.' Cracks began to appear and Rackham also had doubts over the adhesive of the bonded subframe with-standing the heat that would be poured into

it by the catalyst, prompting a switch to steel. Although heavier, the steel unit could be made in-house, resulting in significant savings and creating much-needed work for the Lotus fabrication department.

Prototype 2 received hand-made body panels moulded from the styling clay and was taken to MIRA's full-size wind tunnel in June 1995 to see how the aerodynamic tweaks had affected the car's stability, the aerodynamicists' positive reactions coming as a relief to all. Like the first generation Elan, the car took some refining to become a legendary handler. Speaking in *Classic & Sports Car* magazine, Graham Warner found a pre-production Elan tricky when he raced it in 1963. 'At nine tenths it was fine, but that last tenth made it a very difficult car to drive on the limit. Jackie Stewart said it was the most difficult sod of a car he had driven, because there was a sudden dramatic transition from nice steady understeer to dramatic oversteer.' This was a trait shared by the prototype M111s: 'They were very tricky on the limit,' confirmed Gavan Kershaw. 'You've always got the laws of physics working against you with a mid/rear engine car; because it is very light you never exceed front tyre grip so you're always dependent on how much rear tyre grip you can get. With a mid-engined car, oversteer is a key you can unlock at any point. It's a bit like throwing a hammer handle-first, the heavy bit always wants to go in front of the light bit. So it's easier to get oversteer than it is to get a neutral-balanced mid-engined car.' Tony Shute's obsession with light weight also contributed to the odd scary moment, as he admitted. 'I nearly had my biggest accident ever at the Nürburgring in the original car. We tried to run it without anti-roll bars; there is a lot of complexity with an anti-roll bar so why have one? But we did need one, we just could not get the understeer/oversteer balance without.'

Refining the M111's on-road performance was down to the development engineers, including ride and handling guru Dave Minter and Lotus racing legend John

Miles. With a stiff chassis and accurate suspension mountings a testament to Richard Rackham's racing Esprit design experience, the building blocks were in place for a much harder feel than the Elan, a real racer for the road. Testing at Hethel, MIRA, in the heat of the Nardo track in Italy, the varying surfaces and conditions of Millbrook, and not to mention the out-and-out handling test of the Nürburgring in Germany, all helped to refine the M111 driving experience to perfection.

Because of the car's low weight and rear-biased distribution, power steering was unnecessary and the M111 featured superb steering response. It was tuned for a careful balance between low-speed tyre scrub and high-speed stability, with the castor angle altered to give more feedback mid-corner, and stiff suspension bushes to reduce the effect of compliance steer. The choice of suspension for the M111 was obvious – race-style double wishbones, but it was a combination of on-track work and testing on the Lotus Engineering compliance rig that helped engineers tune the car's suspension for the traditional Lotus balance of ride and handling. Weight watching once again, the team chose lighter but costlier monotube dampers over the traditional twin-tube option, with inverted mounting to reduce unsprung weight. The difficulty with the single-valve monotube is that compression and rebound cannot be altered separately, so tuning the damper to reduce roll is likely to signal poor ride quality. This conundrum was solved by a set-up combining a wide track and stiff dampers, to give secure cornering and limited roll, with relatively soft co-axial coil springs to give good ride quality and toe-out in compression to reduce the effect of mid-corner bumps.

Having used Bilstein dampers on the first prototype, the engineers opted for Dutch Konis for production, trying a variety of settings with different valving in conjunction with tyre testing. Vehicle dynamics engineer Gavan Kershaw explained the results of tyre

testing at MIRA and Nardo. 'Because the Elise was designed to have off-the-shelf tyres we tested most of the tyres on the market and picked the best rear and the worst front, because you want a bit of natural understeer.' Having settled on the Pirelli P Zero, with 185/55 R15 fronts and 205/50 R16 rears, the engineers then had to put further load into the forward tyres to dial out the inherent oversteer, setting higher spring rates up front and adding an anti-roll bar.

Breakthrough in braking

Much to Tony Shute's frustration, the nearer the M111 got to production, the more weight it gained. The 'Step-in car' target of 575kg (1,268lb) had been increased to 650kg (4,229lb) when the decision was made to add doors and roof, but the search was on to lose weight wherever possible. In tandem with the ride and handling development, Lotus engineers worked in association with American firms Lanxide Corporation and

The M111 was the first production car to feature metal matrix composite aluminium and ceramic discs, shown off by slender Lotus-designed five-spoke alloy wheels shod with Pirelli P Zero tyres. (Tony Baker)

The no-compromise attitude of Ducati and the pride of ownership instilled by its 916 superbike inspired the Lotus designers and engineers. (Ducati)

Like the Elise, the Ducati 916 offers tantalising glimpses of its structure, which is as beautiful as the bike itself. (Ducati)

Hydraulics Inc to make the Elise the first production car to feature metal matrix composite (MMC) brake discs. Previously only seen in racing cars, the MMC disc was a blend of aluminium and ceramics, made by reinforcing the metal with 20 per cent silicone carbide. When allied to lightweight pads the discs saved some 12kg (26.5lb) unsprung weight, and were also another saleable technology for Lotus Engineering. The challenge was to develop them to the stage where noise, braking effort and wet weather performance were suitable for road use.

Early difficulties included discs cracking, prompting a switch to a swan-neck design with the rotors ventilating the opposite way to a conventional disc, drawing air from the visible outer side to reduce thermal stress around its mounting face at the hub. The choice of pad was critical, as ride and handling engineer Matt Becker explained: 'It was the interface between pad and disc that gave the friction and the pedal feel. They take

quite a long time to bed in, but in effect the disc never wore down, it actually expanded with the transfer layer from the pad to the disc.' Although the surface of an MMC disc will start to melt some 250° lower than the 700° C of a cast-iron rotor, the heat dissipation of the aluminium compound is so good that it is a temperature the disc is never likely to approach.

The development team put prototypes through aggressive fade tests at Hethel and Millbrook, repeatedly accelerating to 80mph (129km/h) then braking to 20mph (32km/h). But as the ultimate proof of MMC, the team went to Italy in September 1995 to tackle the numerous hairpins of the legendary Stelvio Pass. Astonishingly, the brake fluid didn't boil and the pedal retained feel, a graphic demonstration of the MMC disc's ability. But the big disadvantage was cost. Each disc was sand cast by Lanxide and machined by Hydraulics Inc using diamond tooling, the payoff being that the rotor was predicted to last the life of the car, or at least 100,000 miles. When allied to a Lotus/AP Racing front caliper and a Brembo rear, the braking system offered 1.2g stopping force, yet the pedal feel was so good that the car could do without a servo, saving further weight. The corrosion-free MMC disc also looks great, a fact not lost on Lotus Design who penned the Elise's slender five-spoke alloy wheels, made in Wales by Alloy Wheels International, to show off the discs' beauty.

While work on braking, ride and handling progressed, the purchasing department set out to source affordable but effective parts to put the M111 into production. They say the Devil is in the details, but with a Lotus it's about hiding where those details come from. The Vauxhall steering column and stalks are recognisable, but it's harder to spot that the chunky dashboard switches are lifted from the Peugeot 306, or the headlights from a Renault 4. More amazing are the neat door mirrors; they look just right and actually come from a Metro, the hubs coming from the same source. With the accent on light weight, addenda such as door

Ducati 916: the two-wheeled Elise?

While Elise styling is clearly influenced by the illustrious history of Lotus Cars, the philosophy is based on the products of Italian manufacturer Ducati, and in particular its 916 superbike. Chassis designer Richard Rackham and head of design Julian Thomson are good friends and both were Ducati owners at the time of the project's inception. 'We were single and spent all of our money on toys,' explained Rackham. 'The 916 was hugely different to previous Ducatis, it was designed by guys from Cagiva and was totally breathtaking in its approach to motorcycle design.'

Ducati's 916 engine dated back to an 851cc four-stroke created in 1986, a unit that would sire some of the greatest ever high-performance twin-cylinder motorcycles. Featuring a 'desmodromic' valve system, with four valves per cylinder, it powered Ducati to a dominance of the World Superbike Championship throughout the 1990s. The 916 itself arrived in 1994, powered by a water-cooled 916cc version of the longitudinal 90° V-twin. For 1997,

capacity rose to 996cc for the 916 SPS, giving more power even than a standard Elise with 123hp at 9,500rpm. Delivered through a six-speed gearbox, the Ducati's performance was exhilarating, and it had chassis dynamics and stopping power to match.

Like Lotus, racing heritage, performance and handling are key to Ducati appeal and Rackham and Thomson appreciated the combination of thoughtful detailing and no-compromise attitude. A philosophy of pure driver appeal and aesthetic perfection creates a pride of ownership that the Lotus men wanted to emulate in Project M111. 'It was very refreshing,' Rackham continues, 'all of the technology was visible and clean and functional. It was a great inspiration for the Elise, always there as a driver for the design of the vehicle.'

'Ducatis are extremely purist and beautifully designed and engineered,' said Thomson, 'the important thing was that it really did blur the line between engineering and design.' This combination reappears in the delicate detailing of the Elise, such as the extruded pedal box and suspension uprights. The 916 offers tantalising glimpses of the elegant spaceframe visible behind its carbon-fibre panels, a feature neatly repeated in the Elise, open the doors and you'll see a reminder of the

chassis in the exquisite door hinges. The Ducati helped the design team to look forward, despite retro cues in the Elise styling. 'Although the Elise was supposed to be a modern-day Lotus Seven, we couldn't think of it that way because the Seven was front-engined, designed using entirely different materials and entirely different criteria for safety and technology,' says Rackham. 'So the Ducati was a great example to base our work upon.' It also provided some inspiration for the marketing men at Hethel, as Rackham explains: 'I think it also made a lot of sense that the Elise followed the Ducati marketing example. The base model comes out, then there is an engine upgrade and all the go-faster bits become available, it's that sort of toy.'

But it was the Ducati attitude as much as anything that inspired Lotus to banish its past demons. 'The Japanese had taken over the motorcycle industry in the '70s,' Thomson explained. 'Companies like Ducati and Harley-Davidson tried to be all things to all people and they lost out; they couldn't achieve the thoroughness the Japanese can. We saw the same things happening in the car market and then we saw how Ducati and Harley had resurrected themselves in the last few years by going back to core values.'

handles and interior trim could be designed out, while the steel wishbones, composite windscreen surround and compact heater were produced in-house. The tail lights and front indicators look different, but are the same moulding, just different tints. Resolving and sourcing a single wiper, preferred because it was lighter, cheaper and retained the sports prototype looks desired by the designers, proved difficult.

Independent specialists were unable to achieve the legally required wiped area with such a strongly curved screen. Richard Rackham proved it could be done with a dummy screen and a Citroën AX motor, tilting the spindle towards the screen to ensure the blade remained in contact throughout its arc.

In all, some 12 prototypes were built, including those used for crash testing, but it

Finally bearing a proper name, the Elise show car is ready to wow the crowds at motor shows around the world in 1995. (Lotus)

was Prototype 3 that showed the project team what they had created. Hand-finished in silver and fitted with headlamp cowls, the car even sported badging, with curling script reading 'One Eleven' on the tail. The car was close to going on sale with the name – Lotus was even rumoured to have bought the number plate M111 LCL (Lotus Cars Ltd) for its press fleet. But, as Tony Shute recalled, it wasn't even the original model designation: 'It was Project 112 when it started and we wanted 111 because the name of the car was possibly going to be 'One-Eleven'. A Lotus Formula One car was 111 and we swapped over.' But Elise it

became, named after Romano Artioli's granddaughter, who was born around the time the project started. 'To get a name that you can register worldwide is actually very difficult,' Shute continued, 'we went through the whole company and came up with nothing. He came along and said "Elise", and everybody loved it.'

As the project neared fruition, the team began to gather components for the first show car, due to be unveiled to the public at London's Earls Court Motor Show in October 1995. But in mid-August, Artioli dropped the bombshell that he wanted it to debut at the Frankfurt Motor Show on

12 September. There was much midnight oil burnt over the four weeks that followed, but the car was – just – finished in time. Shortly after 11am on stand B24, Richard Rackham unveiled his dramatic aluminium chassis; significantly, it appeared before the car, showing the importance of the revolutionary structure both to the Elise, and as an advertisement for Lotus Engineering. 'The whole structure was designed with product design in mind so it would look good as a stand-alone item,' explained Rackham. 'It was supposed to bring business to Lotus, so it was beyond engineering, detail design and finished form were very important.' For the show chassis, Rackham had the suspension parts chromed and had designed a delicate display frame. And then came the car. Tony Shute and Julian Thomson pulled back a cover bearing the script 'I am Elise' to reveal the new Lotus, complete with Artioli's granddaughter at the wheel, sporting a T-shirt with the same slogan. Although deliveries were not expected until mid-1996, with a price tag of under £20,000 it brought Lotus from realm of the dream car to within the reach of the common man, and the stand was inundated with buyers wanting to place deposits. The Lotus Elise had arrived.

Publicity material for the Lotus Elise at the 1995 London Motor Show revealed designer Julian Thomson's preferred, unadorned tail styling. (Lotus)

2 The Elise is born

The Frankfurt show car may have looked finished, and good enough to find homes for the first 18 months of production before the 1995 show circuit was over, but there was still work to be done. In fact, the first Elise customer would not receive his car for nearly a year after the model's unveiling.

In early 1996 there were two prototypes undergoing intensive durability testing at Millbrook to make sure the chassis could cope with the worst road surfaces and climatic conditions a prospective owner could throw at it, to insure against expensive warranty claims. Ride and handling engineer Dave Minter returned to Millbrook in March

to set official 0-60mph and top speed figures, beating computer estimates with 60mph (96.5km/h) hit from rest in 5.81 seconds and a 127mph (204km/h) maximum on the high-speed bowl. During the same month, Minter and colleague Matt Becker, together with Tony Shute and senior technician Keith Hare, took two cars for a four-day, 2,500km (1,550-mile) trip to Chamonix for winter testing. Having lived with the car, Shute recommended some detail changes, but was very happy overall. 'It's actually a remarkably practical car, it's a lot more comfortable than you'd expect and it's good on motorways, you feel very safe.'

A close-up shows the impressive performance of the composite crash structure after the 30mph head-on crash test at the Millbrook proving ground. (Lotus)

In May came the hurdle of Type Approval, with Lotus one of the first manufacturers to qualify for all of Europe in one hit, electing to be examined at the RDW Testing Centre in Holland. One advantage of using an off-the-shelf power unit was that it had already undergone emissions certification, and there was further good news when the Elise passed its 30mph (48km/h) head-on crash test back at Millbrook with flying colours. 'Normally cars are wrecked,' explained Shute, 'but it just hit the barrier and rolled back, we could have stuck a new crash structure on the front and driven it home. I've never seen that in a 30mph test before, it was amazing.' When the examiner's concerns, such as sharp windscreen edges, had been satisfied, the Elise was issued its coveted certificate, with Japanese and Australian market approvals following later.

Back at Hethel, production was being delayed by problems in sourcing parts, and last-minute detail design changes. But by April, there were seven pilot-build cars in progress so that the build sequence could be worked out and assembly line operators trained to produce the car. Life was moving even less smoothly at Hydro in Denmark

though, where progress on the new chassis manufacturing plant was slow, and the lack of quality control was concerning Lotus quality assurance engineer Peter Wainwright, sent out to monitor chassis production. With both the Elise and Renault's Sport Spider taking shape at the same time, Hydro was having trouble delivering, not to mention difficulties with the extrusions themselves, which were suffering from discoloration and imperfections. However, both speed and quality of production steadily improved and in June the firm looked to have cracked it.

By mid-1996, Group Lotus had been up for sale for nearly a year as owner Bugatti Industries had suffered financial difficulties. Just weeks before the first Elise was due to be delivered, four directors and the company secretary confronted Romano Artioli to force the pace of the sale, receiving suspensions for their trouble. As 1996 drew to a close, Malaysian manufacturer Proton, part of the DRB HiCom group, which also owned Petronas (Perusahan Otomobil Nasional Berhad), purchased a major stake in Group Lotus. The much-needed injection of cash gave the firm its most stable foundation for

The Elise wing mirror was sourced from the Rover Metro, but a neat mounting bracket made it look part of the car. (Tony Baker)

How to *build an* *Elise*

Morris Dowton, a Lotus man since the Cheshunt days, was head of manufacturing for the original Elise. He recalled how the car was made ready for production in record time: 'One of the reasons it was so quick was the integration of the manufacturing guys with Tony Shute's team to help develop the car. The first pilot and pre-production cars were put together in Engineering, then, when we got to the first production runs, we had the layout of the new line in position.' Dowton cited teamwork as the reason the Elise could be turned to a full production car from its original planned total of 2,700 units. 'If we've got to, we do eight days a week and 25 hours a day to get the job done. When we started manufacturing the car to the original concept we were building 15 a week, and it was a constant climb on more tooling because the success was a lot more than we anticipated. Not only did we turn it around to 3,000 units a year, but we got up to 3,000 units faster than we ever had before. It was so successful that every time we made a car it had to go out. At our very best we were producing Elises for urgent customers in three days and I believe that is world class for a composite-bodied niche vehicle.'

Building an Elise was almost like putting together a giant Meccano set, more assembly than construction, but the factory was keen to maintain the quality standards reached during production of the M100 Elan, gaining the QS 9000 quality management rating in 1998.

The complex front and rear clamshells of the Elise required a return to labour-intensive 'hand-lay', much to the frustration of the manufacturing team. This entailed first spraying a gel coat finish into the mould to give the panel its smooth surface. The correct grades of glassfibre matting were then cut from templates and laid in before skilled operatives brushed resin on and laboriously smoothed the surface with a hand roller to remove air pockets. Each mould was made up of different sections, which were then unbolted to release the panel to be sent for baking and air curing before a second visit to the oven. Although patchy quality can be a drawback to hand-lay, the finish of the Elise was very good, with none of the kit-car feel that glassfibre can acquire. 'Hand-lay is pretty crude,' admitted Tony Shute, 'but the tooling cost is quite low and you can change it right at the end of the programme. When you're doing a two-year programme you get stuck into doing things like that.'

Some panels, such as doors, bonnet, windscreen frame and sills, could be made using the quicker and less labour-intensive VARI (vacuum assisted resin injection) process, developed for the 1974 Elite. This method involves spraying the gel coat on to a female mould, laying the matting and then fitting a male mould and creating a vacuum into which liquid resin can be injected. The stronger crash structure was made by the more costly high-pressure resin transfer moulding (RTM) system. Once a set of panels had been produced it was taken to the machining area where a high-power water jet trimmed imperfections and cut apertures such as the headlamp holes. After final tidying by hand the panels then moved to the paint shop to be primed, painted and lacquered then baked in an oven to cure the finish. A check for blemishes under daylight inspection lighting was made before they could be sent to the assembly line.

Early chassis production was at the Hydro plant in Tonder, southern Denmark, but from 1998 it transferred to the new Hydro factory in Worcester, reducing costs and complications. The construction process and bonding techniques were conceived by Lotus, but carried out by the experts at Hydro. Once the aluminium had been extruded and machined, it was anodised to pre-treat the surface before the adhesive was applied and the structure assembled in a jig. The bonds were executed in a controlled environment with careful monitoring of temperature and humidity to ensure every bond was perfect, before the rivets could be applied and the structure removed from the jig for the adhesive to be oven-cured. Steel parts such as wishbones and rear subframes were machined at Hethel, with pressings stamped by computer-controlled tools and welded in jigs by trained operatives, before being sent away to be zinc galvanised.

Lotus-made and sourced parts met the chassis in the assembly area, more a progressive coming-together of components than the automated approach of motor industry big boys. The chassis was mounted in a rotating frame and first the wiring loom, then the steering rack, pedal box, handbrake, gear linkage and fuel tank and lines were fitted. Once the rear subframe was in place the K-series engine could be lowered in and the suspension, brakes and roll bar added. Next, the glue came out again to bond in the crash structure, windscreen and body, which aligned on special pick-ups designed-in as part of the extrusions. The clamshells themselves were fitted with lights and grilles on a sub-assembly before meeting the chassis.

With the body in place, the suspension was aligned, a job made significantly easier by the Hunter rig, which accurately aligned the wheels using hub-mounted sensors. The in-house moulded doors and seats, as well as soft-tops and vacuum-moulded plastic parts, were hand-finished in separate sub assemblies before being fitted on the line. Once completed, the car was checked over, fired up and taken for a shakedown on the track before being tested for leaks. Twice a week, a car was selected at random to be given a full quality audit both in the factory under the daylight quality lights and out on the track to ensure standards remained as high as possible.

As further variations appeared on the same basic tub (see Chapters 3 and 5), there was a new challenge for the production team. 'Factory 1 became a more flexible assembly line, introducing 135s, 160s, 111Ss and 340Rs,' recalled Dowton. 'We had to work out different times for different processes for each model. At one time, we were producing 60 cars a week with five different variants on the line; every 30 minutes we'd produce a car. I was so proud of those people and what we achieved during that period of time.'

With the popularity of the Elise and its variants (Exige pictured) the factory was soon working flat out to meet demand. (Virgin Interactive)

A completed Elise undergoes final checks before going out to its new owner. (Virgin Interactive)

some years, while the passionate Lotus fan Artioli retained a 20 per cent share and remained a director.

Despite the wranglings in the boardroom, the first customer car was driven off dealer Bell & Colvill's forecourt on 1 August. A lengthy waiting list soon developed and speculators fortunate enough to get their hands on a car were making a substantial instant profit in a marketplace hungry for a new Lotus. By the end of July, 1,300 people had put down £1,000 deposits, and with the first year's production intended to be just 400 cars, only 200 of which were earmarked for the UK, the decision was made to up production to 2,500 units a year.

The front lights of the Elise mimic the legendary Europa, which was so low that it required the indicators to be moved inside the headlights and up on the bonnet to make them more visible. (Tony Baker)

It was only appropriate that the Europa, the first mid-engined production Lotus and legendary for its superb handling, should provide inspiration for the Elise. (LAT)

In final production form the Elise lost its headlamp cowls, but gained a roll bar cover and hood. (Tony Baker)

Designer Julian Thomson may not have liked the rear spoiler, which looks like an afterthought, but it certainly added aggression as well as downforce. (Tony Baker)

Even with the hood up the cheeky lines of the Elise are pleasing, the roof fitting over the cabin like a tight cap. (Tony Baker)

As well as leaving much of the anodised aluminium structure exposed, designers hinted at the car's advanced construction with a tactile aluminium gear knob. (Tony Baker)

The Elise on the road

Whether you think it's pretty or ugly, there is no denying that the Lotus Elise is a distinctive little car. The combination of modern mid-engined design and cheeky retro looks really works, with Europa-style lights and Elan-style mouth giving a family Lotus look. The Frankfurt show car's styling was altered little before production, only refined with neater mirror stalks, a body-coloured cover for the roll bar and the loss of the stylish headlight cowls. Intended to be offered as an optional extra, the cowls remained on press cars, but they were abandoned after production problems. As the car was offered with a sub-£20,000 price tag, there was money to be made from the options list. Popular additions were metallic paint (£690), leather trim (£585) and front driving lamps (£255). Not that standard equipment was miserly; there was a three-way catalytic converter, immobiliser, and a 12-month unlimited mileage warranty with a further eight-year corrosion warranty on the chassis.

Clamber aboard and the car's step-in origins are obvious from the wide sill, with entry requiring a particular knack when the

A Chapman Lotus? Son of a legend speaks

One observation of the Elise is continually reiterated, that it is a true 'Chapman Lotus', signalling a return to the ideals of Colin Chapman, the founder and – even today – inspiration for Group Lotus. Ironically, the car sold alongside Elise was the Esprit, a car born in Chapman's era, but it is the Elise philosophies of light weight, technical innovation and pure driver appeal that earned an association with the great man. Who better to ask what the old man would have thought than Clive Chapman, son of Colin and supremo of Classic Team Lotus, the firm that keeps some of his father's greatest racing cars alive and competing in historic race series?

Clive and his mother Hazel were given a sneak preview of the Elise before launch, and his reaction was a PR's dream. 'I thought it was terrific,' he said. 'It was certainly in the spirit of a Lotus and the concept of the chassis was really impressive and absolutely what dad would have approved of. The use of materials, the way they are bonded and the design of the structure, so strong and yet so light, is exactly what it's all about, and then things like the extruded uprights were so tasty that I'm sure he would have gone for it.' But it was not all positive. Clive rued the slightly fussy styling which ruled out the use of his father's beloved vacuum-assisted resin injection (VARI) moulding method. 'I don't think he would have approved of the body-work because it was a complicated hand lay-up procedure and dad was very much into the VARI system. He would have wanted something simple, so I don't know whether he would have let the stylists get away with so many swoops and curves and ducts.

'I think he saw the body as the last thing that was done and what was underneath it was the most crucial thing. He would have wanted the body to be as easy to make and as easy to repair as possible.' Not that the stylists are running the show. Clive Chapman believed that, in the best Lotus tradition, the car's technical innovations were still the key to the success of the Elise formula. 'It is elegant and it has been engineering-led,' he explained, 'whereas some other cars in that category are marketing-led or styling-led, I think that's why the Elise is a true sports car. If somebody wants a proper sports car than really they should get a Lotus Elise, whereas if they are making more of a fashion statement then I suppose there are other cars around.'

Clive believed that the variations the Elise spawned (see Chapter 5), could be accused of being folly, but had their uses. 'As a promotional exercise the 340R was a huge success, it got terrific coverage,' he said. 'I don't know what it was like commercially, but in some ways that doesn't matter because it really got Lotus a tremendous amount of positive attention. The Exige was born out of the racing car, but I don't know how practical it is as a road car. That's taking a racing car and putting it on to the road whereas the Elise is coming at it from the production car direction, which is more sensible in some ways.'

Clive was less impressed by the efforts of Lotus on the track in its own one-make series (see Chapter 4), although moves into endurance racing looked promising. 'It's a shame there isn't a world class FIA category where the Elise could compete against other engineering-led designs, because that's what Formula One is and unfortunately Lotus isn't in Formula One any more – that's real racing.'

And how did Chapman sum up the Elise? 'It's a classic in it's own lifetime.'

---

hood is up. But as Tony Shute explained, it's all part of the experience: 'It's a driver's car, the fact that it's difficult to get in and out of is irrelevant because it's just got one purpose in life, it's very focused.' Early cars featured plasticky window winders and the hood design is a real pain until you get used to its complexity compared with, for example, that on a Mazda MX-5. Once inside though, the parts-bin switchgear looks right and feels positive, avoiding a kit-car sensation, and the anodised aluminium surfaces are tactile and attractive.

The Elise is very roomy, with a tiny transmission tunnel compared to backbone chassis cars and none of the claustrophobia of a Europa. An Elise can feel cramped though if the driver's seat is placed well back, when occupants rub shoulders thanks to the perimeter structure pushing them together.

Clive Chapman believes his father, Lotus founder Colin, would have approved of the Elise. (Author)

Simplicity is the key to the Elise interior, which boasts a near-perfect driving position and pedal layout, as well as surprising comfort and refinement. (Tony Baker)

Unclothed, the Renault Sport Spider's welded aluminium chassis is both heavier and less elegant than Richard Rackham's extruded and bonded masterpiece. (Renault)

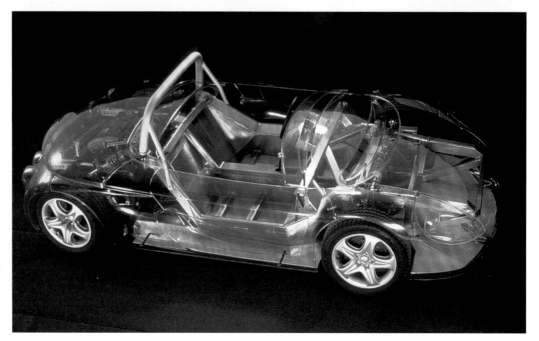

Renault Sport Spider: the French Elise

You can't help but feel sorry for Renault. It unveiled its dramatic new Sport Spider with a flourish, only to have its thunder comprehensively stolen by a little British roadster called Elise. The Sport Spider first appeared, in racing form, at the 1995 Geneva show, with the road-going version arriving a year later.

In a lot of ways the Renault and Lotus are very much alike. Both were spartan sports cars with no compromise to comfort; in fact, with no hood and originally no windscreen, the Renault was nearer to the step-in concept originally conceived for Elise. The two cars' philosophies were also very similar, with aluminium chassis, simple interior, composite bodywork and compact transverse mid-mounted 16-valve four-cylinder engine. Both offered an exciting driving experience with excellent roadholding, and in the UK there was even the Renault Sport Race Series for the Sport Spider supporting the British Touring Car Championship, a role the Sport Elise would later repeat (Chapter 4).

One major difference lay in Renault being such a large company that it could borrow components from its own parts bin, rather than forming partnerships with other companies. A Clio Williams engine was fitted and the Spider was built at the Renault-owned Alpine factory in Dieppe, very appropriate for this comparison as Alpine is a firm often seen as France's answer to Lotus, with innovative plastic-bodied sports cars using off-the-shelf power plants and backbone chassis.

Compared with the Elise, the Sport Spider is a real heavyweight, crushing the scales at 940kg (2,073lb), over 200kg (440lb) more than the Lotus. Much of this weight difference is due to the chassis construction. While both cars employ aluminium chassis and were developed – in parallel, yet in secrecy – and built by Hydro Aluminium Automotive Structures, the Renault's lattice frame was welded together after Renault engineers failed to discover the secret of bonding aluminium, as exploited by Richard Rackham's team of engineers. And it cost more too: at £25,950 in 1997 it was a whole £7,000 more than the Elise. OK, so it had more power, its 1,998cc 'four' producing 150bhp at 6,000rpm and propelling it to an impressive 134mph (216km/h) maximum, 10mph (16km/h) greater than the Elise. There were the same double wishbones and coils all round, and the Renault's wider tyres (205/60 front and 225/50 rears to the Elise's 185/55 front and 205/50 rear) and extra track should spell handling that's

every bit as good. But its extra beef meant it lagged nearly 1.5 seconds behind the Elise on the all-important 0–60mph dash, at 6.9 seconds.

Production of the Sport Spider ended at the turn of 1999, after less than three years, and while it was never intended as a full-scale production model, there is no doubt that it never stood much of a chance after the arrival of the Elise. Richard Rackham recalled meeting the Sport Spider project manager, Yves Legalle, at the Elise's launch: 'He came on to our stand at Frankfurt when we unveiled the car. The chassis was there and he looked completely dumbstruck. After a few minutes he just walked past me and muttered 'this cannot be'. I talked to him and he told me it was exactly what he wanted for the Renault Spider and the engineers had told him it was impossible. From the look on his face you could tell he realised that the Spider was going to go nowhere.'

And just for extra irony, the Sport Spider was the car that took Lotus evaluation engineer Alastair McQueen to victory in *Autocar*'s inaugural Sideways Challenge in 1998, the first of four consecutive wins for Elise test drivers in the competition. 'It had a lot of grip and more power than the Elise, but it was also heavier,' McQueen recalled. 'Cornering capability was higher, but actual performance was not much different because it's all about power to weight: if you don't have a lot of weight to drag around you don't need a lot of performance to do it.'

Renault's Sport Spider (pictured here is the roadgoing version with windscreen) was trumped by the lighter, faster Lotus. (LAT)

Instrumentation is provided by a clear and effective Stack unit, featuring speedometer, rev counter, digital fuel and temperature gauges and warning lights. (Tony Baker)

Despite offering just 118bhp, the Rover K-series – dressed with Lotus cam covers – perfectly suits the lightweight Elise, offering instant response throughout the rev range. The tiny boot is less effective. (Tony Baker)

While magazines may show Elises broadside with smoke pouring off the tyres, the natural – and quickest – cornering pose for the car is exploiting its tenacious grip. (Tony Baker)

One of the few disappointments with the Elise driving experience is the rather dull and unsporting exhaust note, although the race-inspired centre-exit twin pipes look great. (Tony Baker)

The Elise has few direct rivals, but the motoring press inevitably pitch it against softer sports cars such as the MGF and Mazda MX-5. (LAT)

The pilot's seat does move, but the passenger's is fixed in the rearmost position, with a drilled aluminium footrest thoughtfully provided, to give the driver improved room and visibility. On longer journeys, you need to travel light as the compact boot has room only for a couple of soft bags. There are storage pockets beside the gear lever and there is space behind the seats for stowing either the removable rear screen or the hood construction, and once you get used to stowing carefully the Elise is a surprisingly practical proposition. It suffers little buffeting with the hood down and cruises serenely on the motorway, with the greatest surprise being the apparently uninviting seats, which are remarkably comfortable despite little padding, and with their pump-up lumbar support back trouble can be avoided on long journeys.

Appropriately for an enthusiasts' car, the driving position is near perfect for most drivers. The small but chunky leather-rimmed Nardi three-spoke steering wheel is fixed, but the simple Stack instruments behind are easy to read. Slender pedals feel good and are ideally spaced in the roomy footwell for the keen driver. 'The Elise was about being within nice kit,' explained Richard Rackham, 'every part of it which interfaces with your body we really worked on: the wheel's in the right position, you can see out of the car, your feet aren't cluttered.'

The excellent Elise power-to-weight ratio was gained by saving weight rather than offering massive power, which also sharpened steering, braking and handling. The joy of the K-series's installation in the Elise is its torque, which, when allied to superb throttle response, signals a car that always feels eager and alert, and with the engine slung over the rear wheels traction is superb. 'When you get blasted around a track by someone like Tony [Shute] you realise that it's all it needs,' said vehicle dynamics engineer Gavan Kershaw. 'The

weight is the major focus, you do notice it when you've got a passenger, but there's no point chasing 300 horsepower if you can make a car like we do.' The only criticisms of the way the car performs lie in the disappointing exhaust note and the rubbery gear change, which really lacks the click-click precision of a Seven or Type 26 Elan. This problem is inevitable with an indirect gear change operated by a cable linkage, as suffered by the Europa, and it does loosen up as mileages increase.

For any drivers sceptical of the bonded structure, it is a case of 'don't knock it 'til you've tried it', as the confidence it inspires and the ride and handling compromise are just superb. Richard Rackham explained why the Elise chassis is so competent: 'When I joined Lotus in '87 I worked with the ride and handling department, through that process I learned where all the flaws were in passenger cars. I was also the designer attached to put all the changes into our

Esprit to make it into a race car. So I had a background of knowing how to make road cars handle and how to make racing cars go pretty well, which enabled me to go straight to the point on the Elise.'

Ride quality is generally very good, and particularly evident in the way the Elise dismisses mid-corner bumps when a more stiffly set-up car would be heading for the nearest ditch. But it will crash and thump over larger potholes, no great surprise for a car that has just 100mm wheel travel, although the structure always feels stiff and composed. The handling itself is very neutral, but it is possible to persuade the rear end to let go and indulge in powerslides out of lower speed corners. More worrying is a tendency for cars to spin when the limit is reached, or if the driver backs off the throttle in a corner.

The engineers admit that an Elise requires a higher-than-usual skill level to extract the most from it, and on the road the car creates

The car was named Elise after Bugatti boss Romano Artioli's granddaughter. Tail lights and front indicators are all the same moulding, simply different colours. (Tony Baker)

And the winner is . . . the award-winning Elise

Auto Week, Frankfurt 1995: Most Fun Car
Anglia Business Awards 1995: Winner, Innovation Category
The Times: Best Car of the Year 1996
Car Design and Technology Awards 1996: Best Innovation in Production (chassis and brakes)
   Most Innovative Production Car
   Reader's Vote: Best Designed New Car
Autocar: Technical Award 1996 (chassis)
Autocar: Best Handling Car 1996
Performance Car: Performance Car of the Year 1996

European Aluminium Award (Automotive) for Passenger Cars 1996
Sport Auto, Die Sportlichsten Autos 1996: Winner Category C
The Prince of Wales Award for Innovation 1996: Finalist
Auto Express New Car Honours 1997: Sporting Car Honour
Sport Auto, Die Sportlichsten Autos 1997: Winner Category C
What Car? Car of the Year Awards 1997: Best Roadster
Top Gear magazine: Top Sports Car 1997
Sport Auto, Die Sportlichsten Autos 1998: Winner Category C
What Car? Car of the Year Awards 1998: Best Open Top Car
Top Gear magazine: Top Sports Car 1998
Sir Henry Royce Memorial Foundation Award for Engineering Excellence 1999
What Car? Car of the Year Awards 1999: Best Open Top Car
Top Gear magazine: Top Sports Car 1999
Sport Auto, Die Sportlichsten Autos 1999: Winner Category C

Sport Auto, Die Sportlichsten Autos 2000: Winner Category C
What Car? Car of the Year Awards 2000: Best Open Top Car
Auto Vum Joer: Design Award 2000
Auto Express New Car Honours 2000: Commended
Auto Express Used Car Honours 2000: Commended
Sport Auto: Drift Challenge 2000
Autocar: Best Driver's Car 2001
Auto Express New Car Honours 2001: Best Roadster
The Design Council Great Expectations Exhibition 2001: British Design Excellence
What Car? Car of the Year Awards 2001: Second place, Best Roadster Award
Autocar Top 100 Performance Cars of All Time, 2001: Ninth place
Classic & Sports Car Best Ever Lotus poll, 2002: Second place

Enthusiasts fell in love with the Elise, as did the motoring press, which bestowed numerous awards on it for innovation, looks and driver appeal. (Tony Baker)

such staggering grip that those limits are rarely – if ever – reached, so it is more of a concern for the track day hero. And the grip from those Pirelli P Zeros remains impressive in wet weather too. 'It's a case of trying to maintain the handling balance between wet and dry so it doesn't have a big change in character between the different conditions,' explained evaluation engineer Alastair McQueen. 'Our cars tend to be set up to get more understeer in the wet, which is the safest condition to have.'

It is the quality of complete driver involvement and the purity of signals through the seat and wheel that make the Elise such a great car both on the road and the track. The steering is stunning: light, direct and responsive, rewarding a delicate touch with pinpoint accuracy. Even the brakes, despite a lack of a servo, are excellent, full of feel and with a firm pedal providing the perfect platform for heel-and-toe gear changes. Only the lack of an anti-lock system requires a little more concentration in wet weather.

Part of the early production run was earmarked for press cars, which became available at the end of June 1996. There was no fanfare, no press launch in an exotic location with expensive lunches, as a cash-strapped Lotus Cars saved money and instead let the car do the talking for it. The reaction was astounding, with universal and almost unequivocal praise heaped upon the little roadster.

The eulogies came flooding in, *Car* magazine concluding: 'So fast, so agile, so pure, the 21st century sports car is here now.' *Evo* decided: 'No other car on earth extracts more magic from 118bhp than the standard Elise,' and called it 'the perfect conversion of power into motion. Pure, unsullied, sensational. Nothing with so little weight should feel so effortlessly planted, so untwitchy.' When it went under the scrutiny of the famous *Autocar* Road Test it was in a class of its own, with five stars out of five for ride and handling, economy, and market and finance, four for performance and brakes,

and design and engineering, giving it top marks of five overall. The text was even more positive, praising the designers and extolling the virtues of Lotus engineers: 'It changes the way we will look at and judge the ride and handling of affordable sports cars forever.' The car was marked down for its gear change, dull engine note, a lack of airbags and ABS, and the poor fit and finish of the pre-production example tested. In conclusion, the magazine called the Elise: 'a reference point in the history of the motor car,' with the verdict: 'Rewrites the book on driver appeal.'

When it came to annual awards ceremonies the Elise cleaned up as handling, design and innovation prizes filled the Hethel trophy cabinet. Although they had confidence in the car, the team behind the M111 were taken by surprise by its overwhelming success. 'Everyone who was involved must have been proud of the uniqueness of the car,' said Richard Rackham, 'nothing like that had been done before and it featured on hundreds of front pages of magazines because of its uniqueness, I think that's where the biggest thrill was.'

Inevitably for a car developed in such a short time, there were changes after the Elise had hit the road. At night, the headlights of oncoming traffic hit the rear screen of early cars, ruining rearward visibility, so the rear window was angled to avoid reflections. There were recalls, the most serious of which in 1998 was to rectify bolts working loose in the rear suspension, but the biggest change to the specification was the loss of the lightweight MMC brake discs. In mid-1998, after around 4,000 cars had been built, rotor manufacturer Lanxide Corporation went out of business, forcing Lotus to switch to cast iron and adding to unsprung weight. 'You'll see them coming back in on road cars within a few years,' explained Richard Rackham. 'I guess the world wasn't ready, but unfortunately now when it rains you see rusty stuff through the wheels, the original plan was like a motorbike, to have discs that didn't rust.'

3 Evolution
of the breed

Wonderful though the Elise was, as almost any owner, road tester or car nut kid will testify, there is always room for improvement. Although the car had few direct rivals, save perhaps Noble's M10 or the Tommy Kaira ZZ, there were a number of softer convertibles that could tempt your money away from swelling the Hethel coffers and as these improved so the Elise had to up its game.

Product manager Tony Shute explained how Lotus approached the unenviable task of improving on what was, to many, near-perfection already. 'The car's not going to remain the same forever. To me the Elise is about high performance through low weight, so when people say it needs more power I say you just need less weight. When we launched the car initially a lot of the feedback said you can't launch a sports car with only 120 horsepower, and I was actually more concerned about the 700kg, if we were sat there with 500kg we'd have no problems.' Shute was not the only one looking for a more-minimal Elise; an enquiry from Group Lotus chairman Romano Artioli as to what it would look like without a windscreen led Lotus Design to create the one-off concept Elise Sprint for the 1996 Birmingham Motor Show. Drawings by Julian Thomson and his team show that they would have liked to have gone a bit further with the concept, but with just a matter of weeks to create the car from a training chassis donated for the purpose, changes to the standard Elise had to be fairly limited.

That said, it certainly looked dramatic. The most distinctive aspect was the removal of

the windscreen to be replaced by a wraparound Perspex deflector, instantly shedding 20kg (44lb). Reviving a system pioneered on Lotus single-seaters over 30 years before, and also used on the Renault Sport Spider, the Sprint employed a duct that channelled air beneath the deflector and blasted it upwards to redirect airflow over the driver, like having a windscreen made of air. Other alterations to the bodywork included blacked-out headlamp cowls, a simpler fuel filler cap and buttresses kicking up from the rear of the doors to the roll-over bar, while distinctive 'Sprint' script and racing roundels finished off the titanium silver paint. Inside, the left-hand-drive car was much like a standard Elise as there was little stripping out left to be done, but the seats were replaced with minimal buckets lightly padded with foam rubber, and there was a body-coloured wraparound dashboard.

Despite a good reception from motor show visitors, the Sprint was destined to remain a concept car and was put on display in the Hethel reception area before being relegated to the Lotus museum collection. But that was not the end of the story. While its pared-down ideals eventually led to the extreme 340R (see Chapter 5), the car itself would live on. When Lotus auctioned off its museum cars, the Sprint was bought by Ian Coles, director of Lotus dealer The Haydon Group, and turned from a complete but non-running show exhibit into a road-legal fun car, making its first motive public appearance at the 1999 Goodwood Festival of Speed.

Bringing the Sprint to production was never really a prospect and any stripped-out

The Sport 135 was the first hotted-up Elise to hit the road, this example sporting the stylish and practical new hardtop. (LAT)

variation would require serious development. 'The weight thing becomes pretty difficult to change because of legislation and testing,' said Tony Shute, 'so the power output is another thing to look at.' The first outcome of this new approach was unveiled at the Birmingham Motor Show in March 1998. Tagged Sport 135, the new model was given Single Vehicle Approval, meaning it could only be released as a limited edition of 100 cars, priced at a hefty £28,950. The Sport 135 was the first 'production' hot-rod Elise, and before its arrival enthusiasts had to build their own from the performance options list.

The 135bhp engine was created from the Special Vehicle Options (SVO) catalogue of parts, with a polished and ported cylinder head, modified cams, a new air filter, an altered engine management system and a great-sounding sports exhaust, all combining to liberate an extra 17bhp, achieved

1,000rpm higher at 6,500rpm. There was also an additional 8lb ft (11Nm) of torque, although it came in at a heady 5,000rpm. When allied to a five-speed gearbox with a new set of closely spaced internal ratios to keep the K-series singing and make the most of the increased power, the Sport 135 was a vivid performer, although not sufficiently so to warrant the huge price hike over a standard car. In line with the boost in power came modifications to the braking and suspension, again with limited success. The cast-iron discs were drilled and the suspension was stiffened and lowered, making it an improved track car, but with a more harsh reaction to imperfections in the road, spoiling the superb ride and handling balance, one of the greatest qualities of the standard car.

Outwardly, the limited run of special edition cars were identifiable by their silver paintwork, dynamic 'Sport 135' decals on the sides ahead of the rear wheelarches, and the new, five-spoke alloy wheels. Up front the tyres were the same section as the standard Elise, but the rears were widened from 205 to 225 section for increased rear grip. To make it feel a bit more special inside there were superbly shaped Corbeau competition seats and an Alcantara-trimmed version of the handsome Lotus-Nardi three-spoke sports steering wheel. If you missed out on the limited run of Sport 135s, Lotus SVO offered the 135 engine conversion and all the goodies as an option pack for standard cars, which could be fitted during build or as a kit of parts fitted by local dealers. For many this was the best combination, combining the additional grunt and the close-ratio 'box with the excellent ride of the standard suspension set-up.

Another addition to the Elise options list for 1998 was an elegant and effective hardtop. Although the M120 coupé was canned in the same year, the addition of the hardtop, particularly if specified as finished in body colour, gave the Elise an attractive baby coupé look. The new lid boasted an elegant shape, mimicking the line of the hood and stretching over the cockpit like a tight-fitting cap, covering the roll-over bar and sporting tapering tails that merged into the flying buttresses as they sloped down either side of the engine bay. Made from glassfibre, the hardtop was formed using Colin Chapman's pioneering VARI system, a quicker and less labour-intensive method than the hand-lay used to create the front and rear clamshells of the Elise. It was available finished in primer, in black, or in body colour and could be ordered as an optional extra on a new car, priced at £1,275, or through dealers as an accessory.

Power to the people

The best, and certainly most popular, of the factory-fettled Elises was the superb 143bhp 111S. Launched to a fanfare at the March 1999 Geneva Motor Show, the 111S revived the 'One-Eleven' tag, type number and one-time proposed name for Elise, with an 'S' for Sprint, the pre-production moniker for the more powerful version. That extra power came easily with the long-awaited insertion of the variable valve control (VVC) version of Rover's 1.8-litre K-series engine, a unit which had been available in the top-of-the-range MGF since its 1995 launch. But it was not just a more powerful engine in a standard car, although modifications were kept to a minimum to avoid spoiling the recipe that made the original car such a success. 'The two cars were fundamentally the same,' said evaluation engineer Alastair McQueen, 'but we did offer a sports suspension package, which had slightly stiffer springs and revised damping.'

Cross-drilled discs were added all-round to improve the stopping power in line with the 25bhp power boost. In addition to the VVC head, the revised unit boasted larger inlet and exhaust valves, a new aluminium inlet manifold and a revised plenum chamber to improve breathing. There was full sequential fuel injection with adaptive control, and distributorless ignition with individual coils for each cylinder. While it may sound like a gimmick, the variable valve control system was actually a very neat piece of engineering, adding power without the on/off delivery of a turbocharger. Using the same 1,796cc alloy block as the 118bhp K-series, the 143bhp unit boasted a re-engineered head to accommodate the VVC system. Unlike a conventional engine with fixed-valve operation, the VVC head allows the engine to be tuned to give more top end power without destroying torque lower down the rev range by creating a continuously variable cam lobe profile. This altered the duration of the inlet valve opening and its phasing according to engine speed and loading, giving improved power throughout the rev range. The complex system was controlled by an advanced engine management system, giving its 143bhp at a heady 7,000rpm, yet also boosting torque, by some 6lb ft (8Nm), although admittedly the system is not foolproof as the additional torque is not reached until 4,500rpm.

One of a number of similarities with the

More extreme was the
Elise Sprint
demonstration car,
although this Julian
Thomson sketch shows
that the designers
wanted to take it further
than funds would allow.
(Lotus)

When Rover finally gave
Lotus its K-series engine
with variable valve
control and 143bhp, the
Elise 111S was born,
pictured at Hethel with
ride and handling
engineer Matt Becker at
the wheel. (Lotus)

The rivals
that rang **the** *changes*

Alfa Romeo Spider Twin Spark
Price: £23,589 (1999)
Engine: front-mounted 1,969cc in-line four, 155bhp, 138lb ft (187Nm), front-wheel-drive
Top speed: 131mph (211km/h)
0-60mph: 8.4sec
Consumption: 28mpg (10 litres/100km)
Those after a driver's car were disappointed by the soggy Alfa's appalling scuttle shake, but it looked attractive and offered a bit of practicality with open-top fun.

BMW Z3 2.2i Sport
Price: £23,230 (2001)
Engine: front-mounted 2,171cc in-line six, 168bhp, 125lb ft (169Nm), rear-wheel-drive
Top speed: 139mph (224km/h)
0-60mph: 7.9sec
Consumption: 30.7mpg (9.2 litres/100km)
The huge-selling Z3 may be the poseur's favourite and the BMW straight-six engine sounds glorious, but its uncommunicative chassis and steering make it a poor sports car.

Caterham Seven
Price: £20,200 (2002)
Engine: front-mounted 1,796cc in-line four, 140bhp, 124lb ft (168Nm), rear-wheel-drive
Top speed: 120mph (193km/h)
0-60mph: 5.3sec
Consumption: n/a
The original spartan sports car, dating back to 1958 and built by Caterham Cars since 1973. Roadsport SV140 shares Elise K-series engine, light and super-quick but lacks comfort.

Caterham 21 Supersport
Price: £25,520 (1998)
Engine: front-mounted 1,588cc in-line four, 138bhp, 115lb ft (156Nm), rear-wheel-drive
Top speed: 131mph (210km/h)
0-60mph: 5.8sec

Consumption: n/a
Caterham spent years developing the grown-up Seven, but despite being attractive, fast and fun it was quashed by the Elise in the marketplace.

Honda S2000
Price: £28,545 (2000)
Engine: front-mounted 1,997cc in-line four, 237bhp, 153lb ft (207Nm), rear-wheel-drive
Top speed: 147mph (236.5km/h)
0-60mph: 5.6sec
Consumption: 28.5mpg (10 litres/100km)
This high-revving Honda was powerful, comfortable and offered real thrills from its classic rear-wheel-drive chassis. But it was not cheap, and bettered by the Porsche Boxster.

Mazda MX-5 1.8i
Price: £17,495 (2001)
Engine: front-mounted 1,839cc in-line four, 146bhp, 124lb ft (168Nm), rear-wheel-drive
Top speed: 125mph (201km/h)
0-60mph: 8.2sec
Consumption: 32.5mpg (8.7 litres/100km)
The car that should be credited for kick-starting the affordable sports car phenomenon. Reliable, fun to drive and with styling inspired by the rear-wheel-drive Lotus Elan.

Mercedes SLK 200 Kompressor
Price: £26,390 (2000)
Engine: front-mounted supercharged 1,998cc in-line four, 161bhp, 170lb ft (230Nm), rear-wheel-drive
Top speed: 138mph (222km/h)
0-60mph: 8.2sec
Consumption: 29.4mpg (9.6 litres/100km)
Pretty and clever coupé/cabriolet more about posing than performance, but a rival for those who bought an Elise as a status symbol. Automatic transmission the norm!

MGF 1.8i VVC
Price: £20,670 (1999)
Engine: mid-mounted 1,796cc in-line four with variable valve control, 147bhp, 128lb ft (173Nm), rear-wheel-drive
Top speed: 131mph (210km/h)
0-60mph: 7.6sec
Consumption: 36.3mpg (7.8 litres/100km)
Hydragas suspension gave the MGF a

good ride, but it felt like a roofless Rover 200. More power from VVC engine, but the K-series is better exploited in the lightweight Lotus.

Noble M10
Price: £27,900 (1999)
Engine: mid-mounted 2,544cc Ford V6, 168bhp, 162lb ft (220Nm), rear-wheel-drive
Top speed: 147mph (236.5km/h)
0-60mph: 5.9sec
Consumption: 25.4mpg (11.1 litres/100km)
Unhappy styling was the only thing between this low-volume car and success for some, although it is no featherweight Elise. Powerful and fine handling, but short-lived.

Porsche Boxster
Price: £34,095 (1997)
Engine: mid-mounted 2,480cc flat six, 204bhp, 206lb ft (279Nm), rear-wheel-drive
Top speed: 139mph (223.6km/h)
0-60mph: 6.5sec
Consumption: 27mpg (10.5 litres/100km)
The almost-rival for the Elise that was always a price bracket above. The arrival of the 111S brought Lotus close, with the faster Boxster S seen as a rival for the Elise-based Exige (see Chapter 5).

Tommy Kaira ZZ
Price: n/a
Engine: mid-mounted 1,998cc in-line four, 185bhp, 142lb ft (192Nm), rear-wheel-drive
Top speed: 140mph (225km/h)
0-60mph: 4.8sec
Consumption: n/a
Superb performance and handling meant this Japanese flyweight could have been a contender, but gawky styling, poor marketing and the Lotus Elise killed it off in Europe.

Toyota MR2
Price: £18,495 (2000)
Engine: mid-mounted 1,794cc in-line four, 138bhp, 125lb ft, rear-wheel-drive
Top speed: 126mph (202.7km/h)
0-60mph: 7.5sec
Consumption: 37.2mpg (7.6 litres/100km)
Cheaper, softer, heavier and slower, but a similar idea to Elise and even has a hint of the Lotus styling about it, along with strong Porsche Boxster overtones.

Left: Alfa Romeo Spider. (LAT)

Right: BMW Z3. (Author)

Left: Caterham Seven. (LAT)

Right: Caterham 21. (LAT)

Left: Honda S2000. (LAT)

Right: Mazda MX-5. (LAT)

Left: Mercedes-Benz SLK. (LAT)

Right: MGF. (LAT)

Left: Noble M10. (LAT)

Right: Porsche Boxster. (LAT)

Left: Tommy Kaira ZZ. (LAT)

Right: Toyota MR2. (LAT)

limited-edition Sport 135 is the use of the close-ratio version of the Rover five-speed gearbox. First and second gears were raised and the long-legged fifth gear of the original was shortened to bring the ratios all a lot closer together, while the final drive was modified from 3.94 to 4.20. These alterations served to keep the higher-revving engine in its peak power band, so ensuring the extra performance was fully exploited and the peaky K-series always remained on-song, right up until the rev limiter kicked in at 7,200rpm. McQueen explained the decision to use the close-ratio gearbox: 'In initial evaluation of the 111S we ran the VVC engine with a standard gearbox with standard ratios in it and that really didn't work too well, it was a little bit disappointing. We obtained a close-ratio 'box from Rover and suddenly the car came alive by the gearing being more matched to the engine characteristics.'

The 111S was visually very similar to a standard car, with the most obvious identifying feature being a slightly clumsy wing added to the top of the rear lip spoiler

of the original, and a discreet '111S' added beneath the 'Elise' script on the rump. Looking more closely, though, the more observant Lotus enthusiast would start to spot a number of small alterations to create a unique identity for the new, more expensive model. To accommodate the VVC engine, whose valvegear made it slightly taller than the 118bhp version as well as some 7kg heavier, the composite engine cover was redesigned with a neat power bulge. The front end was given a little more aggression with a distinctive 'chip-cutter' grille and standard driving lights, the Perspex headlamp covers of the first show cars were reinstated and the indicators were given smoked lenses, with amber bulbs so that they still flashed orange.

While they appeared very similar to the five-spoke wheels of the standard car, the alloys fitted to the 111S were an all-new slender six-spoke design by Lotus, made by OZ Racing. Like the Sport 135, the front tyres remained as the standard 185s, but the rears were beefed up to 225 section, a new Pirelli P-Zero design developed in

In addition to the extra power, the 111S boasted wider alloy wheels and tyres, improved seats, headlamp cowls and a rear spoiler. (LAT)

conjunction with Lotus engineers with a new construction and compound designed specifically to suit the 111S. The chassis remained unchanged, although the rear track was increased by 12mm and the rear toe-steer angles were revised to suit the broader tyres. To keep the wider tyres legal, the rear arches were flared on their trailing edges with tiny black trims to avoid the expense of altering the rear clamshell.

To make the most of the extra few bhp, Lotus avoided piling on the pounds by not filling the interior with unnecessary luxuries, and the 111S remained just a few kilogrammes heavier than the standard car, the majority of that extra coming from the additional weight of the VVC engine. There were some slightly tacky carbon-fibre effect dashboard inserts, new aluminium winders for the still manually operated side windows, and the dash also wore a badge proudly proclaiming the model number. But the biggest change to the Elise cabin was a pair of revised and much improved leather-covered seats, the design of which was standardised across the range, with deeper foam cushions to add a degree of comfort. The design was neatly executed to avoid altering the hip height of driver and passenger, thus meaning the car still conformed to the H-point homologated for the original car to meet European safety legislation.

Off the line, the higher first and second gear robbed the 111S of a dramatically improved 0-60mph time, but it was clearly quicker once under way, hitting 100mph some three seconds before the standard car, with much improved overtaking potential, demonstrated by a 30-70mph (48-113km/h) time over half a second quicker. Top speed was also raised slightly and, incredibly, economy was as good and in some conditions even better than the car equipped with the 118bhp engine. *Autocar* tagged the 111S 'the friendly Elise' for what it considered safer handling thanks to the wider rear tyres preventing the snap oversteer sometimes suffered by the standard car. Most road testers also rated it very highly as a

track day car, where its rev-happy nature – peak power coming in some 1,000rpm above the standard car's redline at 7,000rpm – could be fully exploited. Listed as a model in its own right, separate to the basic car, the 111S was an instant hit as those who had longed for more power for their Elise finally had an answer from Lotus. That success clearly shows in sales, with more than half as many 111S models built in its first year as standard Elises, despite a £4,000 premium on its purchase price. While that may seem expensive, it was infinitely better value than the more costly and less powerful Sport 135, although the limited edition's rarity should see it hold its value better in the future than the more plentiful 111S. With the popularity of 111S and the ongoing success of the standard car, Lotus Cars production over the 1999-2000 period peaked at over 3,000 units, its highest point since Lotus Cars' most productive time at the turn of the 1970s.

Planning for the future

Of slightly less commercial value, but no less interesting particularly as an indicator of the future for Lotus and the Elise, was the Elise NGV (Natural Gas Vehicle). While all Elises sip fuel where other cars of similar performance guzzle, the NGV was the most environmentally friendly Elise yet, although destined to remain only as a one-off research tool and demonstration vehicle. Created by Lotus Engineering's powertrain team in early 1999, the Elise NGV was developed in association with British Gas as part of the government-funded Power Shift programme. This scheme was designed to concentrate on the use of alternative energy sources, and what better way of bringing the idea to the attention of the public than to create a dual-fuel version of the already high-profile Lotus Elise?

The Elise NGV ran a modified version of the standard 118bhp K-series, adapted to run on both petrol and methane-based compressed natural gas (CNG). The advantages of CNG are manyfold: it is sustainable, runs in near-standard petrol engines and offers very low emissions,

A Julian Thomson sketch of the stillborn M120 Coupé shows how stylish the Rover KV6-powered machine could have been. (Lotus)

cutting carbon dioxide by 30 per cent and other emissions by up to 70 per cent. This feature is particularly useful in the Elise as the K-series unit can suffer from high emissions, one of the reasons why it was not federalised for sale in the USA. The NGV system is a neat installation, with a refuelling point mounted in the engine bay and a 40-litre CNG tank where the standard fuel tank used to be and a 24-litre petrol tank above in the space between the seats and bulkhead. These modifications allowed a standard bodyshell to be used while alterations to the engine were limited to an aluminium VVC inlet manifold in place of the standard plastic item and an extra set of injectors for the CNG. An ECU from a Lotus V8 engine replaced the Rover unit to control both CNG and original petrol injectors.

It was not all good news though, the CNG injectors were noisy and there was a 10-15 per cent reduction in power in the bi-fuel car, not ideal in a performance vehicle with just 118bhp to start with. The extra bulk of CNG also means a petrol car could go 3.5 times further on an equivalent-sized tank. As a performance car, the Elise NGV needed to retain the power of a petrol engine. The clever bit of the Lotus system which set it apart from other bi-fuel cars was that the car started on petrol before switching to CNG when running, but it then switched back to petrol when the driver began to drive hard to give the same maximum power as a standard car, for overtaking etc.

As a sports car manufacturer, Lotus is in a particularly privileged position in having such a rich motor racing heritage to call upon as proof of its performance credentials. The Elise was able to capitalise on those

M120: the coupé that *never was*

There's no doubt that more power was a welcome improvement for the Elise. But for many the baby Lotus would hold more appeal if it didn't leak, was easier to get in and out of, offered a bit more comfort – or even some luggage room. The designers and engineers at Lotus Cars recognised this need, attempting to answer it in 1997 with a concept codenamed M120, the Elise coupé. 'We had a project to design a car that slotted in between the Elise and Esprit,' explained Julian Thomson, 'it was basically a stretched Elise chassis with a V6 engine in it.'

Unlike the stillborn Sprint, Thomson recalled that a running prototype was completed: 'We had a driveable car that I drove and thought was terrific. It was a much more usable car and was much quieter with nicer sound quality. It had fixed hardtop and a big space behind the seats for luggage. It combated some of the Elise problems of no space and not enough power.' For Lotus enthusiasts,

particularly the disproportionately large or those with mobility problems, the cancellation of the M120 in May 1998 was a great loss. The pretty Andrew Hill-penned coupé looked much like a grown-up Elise, with that distinctive nose complete with cheeky face and front-mounted radiator. On paper at least, the coupé also allowed Thomson and his Lotus Design team to reinstate his preferred pert, spoiler-free rear end styling from the Elise concept sketches. 'Roger Becker and his guys said it was too dangerous on the limit,' said Thomson, 'which was probably true with the weight being too far rearward. But it did have much better aerodynamics because it had a much higher tail and a total rear window.' Although it keeps a family resemblance, the tail is substantially different to its soft-top sibling, thanks to a 70mm extension to the rear clamshell to offer a usable boot, accessed by a conventional bootlid, and extra width to house beefier rear wheels. The coupé style offered a tapering roofline, giving a more graceful shape, although there was a hint of aggression from a pronounced rear diffuser and big bore tailpipes. To aid entry and exit it was designed with large doors, the tops of which took a bite out of the roof, mimicking sports racers from the 1960s and '70s

such as the Ford GT40, and the chassis side tubes were lowered (an idea that would reappear in the Elise S2, see Chapter 6).

Offering the torque to make the coupé a more refined cruiser, and retaining the performance without the frenetic revving required with the K-series 'four', the M120 would have reinforced the healthy relationship with Rover by employing its KV6 engine. The wheelbase would have been stretched by 150mm to accommodate the new unit, any possible loss in structural rigidity regained and perhaps even bettered by the addition of a roof. In line with its philosophy as a more luxurious, less wild Elise that you could live with every day, the M120 would boast such niceties as electric windows and air conditioning. But luxury and power came at a price and the M120 was projected to be in the region of £30-40,000, with a less labour-intensive production process allowing up to 3,000 cars to be built annually. However, the further it moved from the original pared-down Elise concept, the further it distanced itself from Lotus philosophy and the project expired, although the theory went on to inspire the M250 coupé concept (see Chapter 9) and the prototype was re-used in the development of the Exige (Chapter 5).

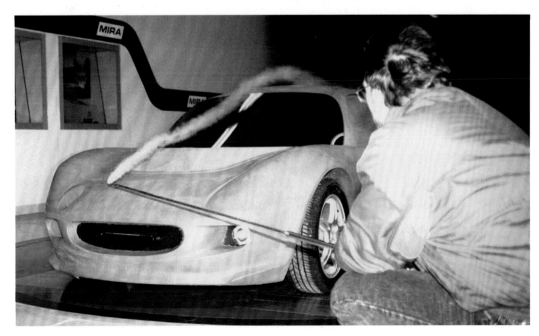

The M120 coupé under the analytical eye of aerodynamicist Richard Hill, in the MIRA wind tunnel. (Lotus)

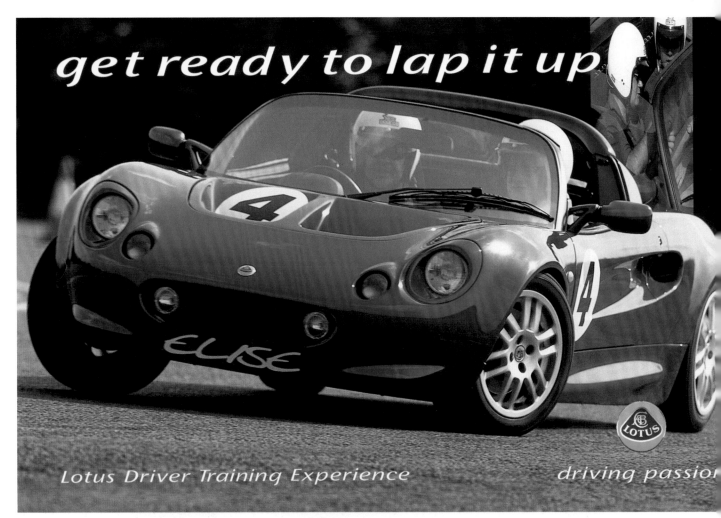

get ready to lap it up

Lotus Driver Training Experience   driving passion

Driver Training was available to individuals and also to large firms for corporate days.(Lotus)

Pioneered by evaluation engineer Alastair McQueen, Lotus Driver Training was a way to teach Elise owners to drive their cars properly, using the remodelled Hethel circuit. (Virgin Interactive)

Lotus Driver Training Experience

With the number of inexperienced drivers going from fairly mundane, mass-produced front-drive cars to the fast and occasionally tricky Elise, Lotus decided it was time to set up a school to teach owners how to get the most from the car. 'It's something we've been looking at for years,' said evaluation engineer and chief instructor Alastair McQueen, 'I devised the course and set it up with my colleague Jonathan Stretton.'

Developed during 1999, the scheme was launched in July and was immediately inundated with enthusiasts wanting to take up the offer to 'Scare yourself sensible'. To make it more suitable for instruction, the 2.25-mile Hethel test track was redeveloped under McQueen's instruction, as he explained: 'This site was a US Air Force base and the original track was laid out in early 1967 using half of two runways and the perimeter track. It was a boomerang shape and had its limitations, we wouldn't be able to train anyone there because it was so fast with no run-offs. After several years of trying we were able

to modify the track and added an infield technical section with three pairs of corners, all of different radiuses with different spacing between them. One of the runways is now a series of curves leading into a fast corner, for driver training the track is quite a challenge for most people, and it's good fun.'

The particular attraction of the Lotus day was the opportunity to benefit from one-to-one instruction from the men behind the cars, such as Matt Becker, Gavan Kershaw and Alastair McQueen from the ride and handling team. Limiting places to 12 per day, the training was very personal, and started out with the option of beginner or intermediate full-day courses, using the restored old clubhouse for hospitality. Days consisted of briefing sessions then track practice in the three standard Elises provided, with demonstrations from the instructors in the afternoon before the trainees were given the opportunity to tackle both the South and Full track, mastering corners such as Chapman, Clark and Graham Hill. Lotus Beginner Driver Training looked into handling, braking and slalom, with Lotus Intermediate Driver Training going into more depth with regard to vehicle dynamics, combining slalom and braking and learning to take corners with oversteer. McQueen explained the success of the course: 'We've been able to provide people with much more enjoyment in the car because they've been able to

understand it, raise the skill level a bit and be more confident.'

As popularity grew, so did the options available, with the addition of the half-day Lotus Elise Experience and Lotus Extreme Experience, the latter adding the opportunity to drive an Exige, 340R and Esprit V8 in addition to the standard Elise. The various activities were also offered as corporate hospitality days and, as the number of days grew, drivers competing in the Autobytel Lotus Championship (see Chapter 4) were added to the list of instructors.

Instructor Gavan Kershaw clarified the difference between the Lotus day and the traditional track driving school: 'What we didn't want to do was to have you turn up and be penalised if you spin, with the instructor next to you having no interest in you. If you can drive very well then he's happy, if you drive badly all he wants to do is survive. We wanted to change that, we want to teach people how to drive, how to correct oversteer, understand what understeer is and what to do if you get it. The car doesn't have ABS so you need to understand braking, slalom, looking ahead, placing the car. We're trying to encourage people all the time, you can spin as many times as you want on our day, as long as after the spin you say: "I know what I've done wrong". That's what we want to hear, we don't say: "Right, back into the pits you've lost your laps", and I think that's why it's been such a success.'

credentials – before creating some of its own with the Sport Elise and the Autobytel Lotus Championship (see Chapter 4) – with a pair of special edition Elises marking the glorious achievements of Colin Chapman and his beloved Team Lotus. These special editions were little more than standard specification Elises, available with 118bhp or 143bhp VVC K-series engines, finished in 'Heritage' colour schemes approved by Clive Chapman's Classic Team Lotus concern. To finish them off there were special interiors and gold-painted 111S-style six-spoke alloy wheels. For the Earls Court Motor Show Lotus displayed the Elise 49, finished in the distinctive 'Gold Leaf' colours of red over

gold over white, as featured on the legendary late-1960s Lotus Type 49 Formula 1 cars made famous by drivers such as Jimmy Clark and Graham Hill. Painting a road car in this scheme was not a new idea as the contemporary Elan Sprint had also been finished in the Gold Leaf colours to celebrate the team's World Championship successes. Inside the Elise 49 were seats trimmed in black leather and red Alcantara, with matching steering wheel. Hot on the heels of the 49 came the Elise 79, marking the Grand Prix successes of the 1970s with a black and gold colour scheme mimicking the 'John Player Special' livery of the great Type 79. As it did when applied to the Europa Twin-Cam

The Elise Type 49 was the first Elise to feature a heritage colour scheme, pictured here with a Lotus 49 Formula One car. (Lotus)

With the 111S came a new badge, reviving the 'One-Eleven' tag that was the original project code for Elise, and was at one point to be its name. (LAT)

Special of the '70s, the scheme really suited the Elise, with a black and yellow interior of similar style to that of the 49. But perhaps the black Lotus badges were inappropriate, as they had previously been worn by Lotus cars to mourn the deaths of Team Lotus favourite Jim Clark and company founder Colin Chapman. Another cosmetic special was the Millennium Edition, celebrating the year 2000 with metallic paint, new alloys and a two-tone leather interior.

A more important new Elise for the millennium was its most powerful roadgoing variant yet, the exciting Sport 160. There was also a 187bhp Sport 190 developed in 1997, but it was very much a car designed for use on the circuit rather than the public highway (see Chapter 4). Much like the earlier Sport 135, whose specification it shared in many details, the Sport 160 began life as a limited edition with only Single Vehicle Approval, limiting its production to 50 cars per year and a total run of 100. However, increased public demand for this most rapid incarnation of the Elise persuaded Lotus to put the car through Full Type Approval, allowing it to be built in unlimited numbers. Early, pre-Type Approval cars can be identified by their vehicle identification numbers, which have an 'F' as their 12th digit, the later cars sporting a 'K' as their fourth digit.

Further tuning of the K-series unit and a new exhaust developed with Janspeed brought peak power up to a handy 160bhp, produced at 7,000rpm, while torque was unchanged from the 111S at 128lb ft (174Nm), although it peaked 500rpm higher at 5,000rpm. When this power was allied to the same, 714kg (1,574lb) dry weight as the VVC-engined 111S, performance was unsurprisingly vivid, with 60mph reached from rest in just five seconds, although top speed was nothing dramatic at 129mph (208km/h). The new car's styling was like a cross between Sport 135 and 111S, with the same stylised decals as the former on the flanks and the latter's tail spoiler adorning the rear. To provide a bit of its own personality, Lotus gave the Sport 160 unique five-spoke MIM alloy wheels, with the same 185 front and 225 rear tyres as the 111S. Mean-looking Scandal Green and metallic black were offered in addition to the full range of Elise colours.

To demonstrate the abilities of its powertrain team, Lotus Engineering built a dual-fuel petrol and natural gas-powered Elise, here demonstrated by Gavan Kershaw. (Lotus)

4 Taking to the track

Just a year after its launch, the Elise took to the track in Italy with the near-standard Trofeo, modified with a roll cage and a Conrero tuning kit.
(Lotus)

Lotus has always been a manufacturer for whom 'racing improves the breed' is gospel – in fact, racing sired the breed. So it was inevitable that the Elise, already competent on track days, sprints and hill-climbs in privateers' hands, should take to the track itself. And it didn't take long.

The first foray into serious racing came soon after the Elise hit the road, with the launch of the Elise Trofeo (Trophy) at the Bologna Motor Show in December 1996. A

demonstration race during the show hailed the arrival of this Italian one-make race series, organised by Peroni Promotions and using essentially standard Elises with the addition of sticky Avon tyres and a Conrero tuning kit, but with the total weight (including driver) limited to 760kg (1,676lb). There were healthy grids for the 1997 season as drivers enjoyed nine rounds of racing at home circuits such as Magione, Misano Adriatico, Vallelunga and Varano,

with an additional race at the Croatian Rijeka track.

Chassis designer Richard Rackham explained why the Elise converted so easily to a racing car: 'It is a very clean aerodynamic shape, the underside is dead flat. The roll-over bar that was in the base car was compliant with RAC regulations and the original cars had extra drillings on the front uprights to take four-pot AP racing calipers – there was also a facility to put racing brakes on the back. Without a doubt this is a little race car for the road or the other way round, it's equally comfortable on both.'

For individuals wishing to go racing with their Elises, there were various options, the most popular being the series offered by the 750 Motor Club and the Aston Martin Owners' Club, with the opportunity to go head-to-head with Renault Sport Spiders, Porsches, TVRs, Morgans and even Aston Martins. The Intermarque Challenge and

Road Sport Series were particularly well supported, in association with Lotus main dealers Bell & Colvill and the Stratton Motor Company. Paul Stokell, a test driver with Lotus Cars Australia, even attacked the legendary Targa Tasmania rally in a near-stock Elise, with only uprated suspension and a sports exhaust. After six days and 2,000km (1,240 miles), the Elise came home third overall and first in class, a major achievement considering the more powerful machinery it was up against.

To give those customers who were serious about racing something a bit more competitive, Lotus developed a very special Elise in time for the October 1997 London Motor Show. A Very High Performance Derivative (VHPD) of the K-series engine featured a modified cylinder head with solid valve lifters allowing it to rev to 8,000rpm. Further modifications, including a carbon-fibre airbox, oil cooler, lightweight competition silencer and exhaust helped the

A number of privateers had a good measure of success before the factory decided to create a dedicated track car. Here, a modified Elise prepared by Lotus dealer Bell & Colvill leads an Aston Martin V8. (Bell & Colvill)

The racing car feel of the Elise meant it was inevitable that owners would take to the track, such as this car in the 2001 Abingdon Sprint. (Author)

new car produce nearly 190bhp, giving the car its name: Elise Sport 190. Intended for track use, but with the possibility of driving to and from the circuit, this 145mph (233km/h) Elise was available as a retro-fit kit for a current car, or could be added during the build of a new car.

It was far from just an engine swap. The suspension was substantially modified with an adjustable anti-roll bar, competition springs and Koni dampers and adjustable spring platforms to reduce the ride height, with the option of a straight-cut Quaife gearbox. The cross-drilled ventilated cast-iron disc brakes boasted race-grade pads, and to look after the driver there was an FIA and RAC-approved roll cage linked to the standard hoop. There were proper racing seats, six-point Sparco harnesses, a plumbed-in fire extinguisher, competition towing eye and battery master switch, while the optional Stack data logging instrument panel could tell you where you were going wrong on the

track. To save weight, the door panels and instrument binnacle were fashioned in Kevlar, there were magnesium alloy wheels shod with Yokohama road/track tyres, and thinner composite clamshells, with the option of up to 50 per cent lighter carbon-fibre items for the super-serious. Just to show what the new car could do, Lotus Engineering product manager Tony Shute couldn't resist getting behind the wheel of the factory demonstrator Sport 190 for a season of hill-climbing in 1997.

But even 190bhp was not enough for some. For Mark Waldron to contest the 1999 British Speed Hillclimb Championship, Lotus built an Elise fitted with a 1400 K-series with a Garrett variable nozzle turbo to produce some 300bhp and 280lb ft (380Nm) of torque. When fitted with an unpainted carbon-fibre body the car weighed just 500kg (1,100lb) and performance was spectacular, with 60mph arriving in a shade over 2.6 seconds, and there was a close-ratio

straight-cut gearbox, limited-slip differential and uprated suspension to cope with all that power.

It wasn't until 1998 that Lotus began to get really serious about racing Elises. Lotus Engineering man Chris Arnold was drafted in to set up and be general manager for Lotus Motorsport Limited, a self-supporting division centred around an all-new Elise racer. 'The Elise is one of the few vehicles you can virtually put straight on to the track with very little modification,' Arnold explained. 'Tony Shute and the guys did a fantastic job of producing something that was useful on the track because it was a quite stiff structure. People were using the Elise for track days, sprints and hill-climbs, and when we set up Lotus Motorsport we wanted to take it a bit further, to give them a car which was more of a circuit racer.' Using the very competent Sport 190 as a basis, Lotus Motorsport set out to create a competitive racer, to be known as Sport Elise.

Just as the Lotus Europa, the first mid-engined Lotus road car and inspiration in many ways for the Elise, had a racing version, the fragile but fast 165bhp Cosworth-powered 47, so the Elise had to be taken further to create an out-and-out racing car. If the Elise is the spiritual successor to the Europa, then the Sport Elise is the modern-day 47, the ultimate incarnation of the model achieved through development on-track.

Like the 47, the Sport Elise needed some visual separation from the standard car, adding some much-needed aggression as well as vital downforce. Chris Arnold recalled: 'For a full track car we had to look quite carefully at aerodynamics, so that meant changes to the front and rear clamshells and front splitters and rear wings. That also gave us the opportunity to toughen it up at the same time. I like the Mk1 Elise, but it's a featherweight and in the middle of a large track it can look a little bit insignificant. I

The Motorsport Elise show car was prototype for the Sport Elise, which was to have a one-make race series for the 200bhp Elise-based racers. (Lotus)

If the Elise was a Europa reborn for the 1990s, so the Sport Elise was a reincarnation of the racing Europa, the Type 47, pictured in 1968 with John Miles at the wheel. (LAT)

Take an Elise, lower it, pump it full of steroids and add some serious aggression and what have you got? The Lotus Sport Elise. (Author)

like to think of the Sport Elise as a Mk1 Elise that's been through the gym for six months.' The new car's bodywork was a collaboration between Lotus Motorsport and Lotus Design, in particular stylist Matt Hill, and the Sport Elise went from sketches to a running prototype in just two months. The first appearance was at the Geneva show in March 1999, with its track debut a demonstration run at the 1999 Goodwood Festival of Speed in June. Its gorgeous lines were pure desire to seasoned petrolheads, pure aggression and pure racer. There was a low front splitter and a Kamm tail with pronounced rear wing to reduce the lift generated by the standard car at high speed. Although still some way off the 700kg (1,540lb) weight target, the 200bhp show car was a vivid performer and demonstrated the potential of the design. Much of the specification of the finished racer was already in place, including a close-ratio straight-cut gearbox, Yokohama slicks, uprated ventilated cast-iron discs with the standard front caliper moved to the rear, and a new four-pot front caliper, developed in association with AP Racing specially for the Sport Elise.

At the prototype's launch, Lotus announced that the new car would compete in its own one-make series, and by the time the completed version arrived at Geneva the following year it was confirmed as the lead support race on the 2000 TOCA tour, behind the headline British Touring Car Championship. There was little to strip out of the already spartan Elise interior, but the driving position was moved to the centre and weight was shaved to hit the 700kg target despite a full firewall and a Safety Devices cage. But, as Chris Arnold pointed out, the chassis remained largely unchanged, even retaining the road car's crash structure and standard uprights and wishbones: 'We didn't change the chassis at all apart from drilling holes to fit roll cages and moving the seat into the centre. It's such a stiff chassis to start with and we've got a six-point cage on top of it as well so it's fantastically stiff. At the end of the day, a road car is tuned to road conditions and it's not part of the sign-off criteria of a road car to thump it over kerbs for 24 hours, so naturally you have to take components and change them for race applications.' The ride height was lowered by some 50mm and competition springs and two-way adjustable dampers were fitted, the car undergoing extensive testing to properly sort the suspension and on-track dynamics before the first season got under way. Over the top was stretched a lightweight composite body, whose style would spawn the stunning Exige road car (see Chapter 5), despite Lotus protestations at launch that a roadgoing version would not be built. In fact, despite its name, the Sport Elise is registered for homologation purposes as an Exige.

Lotus gets back on track

The Autobytel Lotus Championship, as the series would be named after its major sponsor, was unusual in that teams did not buy a car and run it themselves, but instead a driver would buy a season's drive, at £55,000 plus VAT, merely having to turn up on the

For extra braking power, the ventilated discs of the Sport Elise were drilled and grooved and featured a special AP Racing four-pot front caliper. (Author)

Being a pure racing car, the Sport Elise did not require a handbrake so the standard front caliper was moved to the rear. (Author)

For improved weight distribution, the driving position of the Sport Elise was moved to the centre of the car. (Author)

day. Testing, practice, hospitality, engineers and mechanics and even a set of overalls were included in the package, and there were to be prize funds set up for each round. Some 25 cars were built, owned, prepared and maintained by Lotus Motorsport. Former Team Lotus man Chris Dinnage was appointed team manager and there was a 40-strong Lotus Motorsport support team complete with a fleet of Lotus Motorsport-liveried trucks to transport the cars to and from the circuits.

As a further break from the norm, Lotus itself found the major sponsors, with each

Amazingly, the Sport Elise utilised Richard Rackham's chassis in near-standard form, but with a full steel roll cage for the driver's safety.
(Author)

The 2001 Autobytel Lotus Championship grid ready for the off.
(Lotus)

allocated a Sport Elise in its company branding. The sponsors then competed in a 'constructors' challenge', running alongside the drivers' championship, and benefited from corporate hospitality both during race meetings and at Hethel. The original intention was for drivers to be given a different car and race mechanic for each round to ensure no one car was better than the others, but in the end driver, sponsor and car remained together for the season. This consisted of 12 rounds and one non-championship race, 11 supporting the British Touring Car Championship in the UK and Ireland, including a night race at Snetterton, and two 'Lotus on Tour' races in mainland Europe, supporting the FIA Sports Car Series at the Belgian Spa-Francorchamps and German Nürburgring circuits. Each race consisted of 24 minutes plus one lap and the cars were remarkably reliable throughout the season, their identical specification allowing driver skill to shine.

As Chris Arnold recalled, the racing was tight and thrilling to watch: 'We're racing in front of 20–25,000 people and it's difficult not to have exciting racing. It has tended to be a bit kamikaze with a bit more dicing and that's what people like to see. At some circuits the top nine cars would qualify within a second of each other. It does come down to fine tuning of the suspension and a lot of work went into the set-up. We put Stack data logging systems in the car so the drivers can see if they're braking too much for a corner – the cars are so equal on the straight that you can't get it back.' The 2000 season was an impressive success, with more than 20 cars all season, five different winners, and celebrity appearances from *Top Gear*'s Tiff Needell, rally star Gwyndaf Evans, Touring Car ace Will Hoy and even Shane Lynch, from '90s boy band *Boyzone*. Having won the first ever Sport Elise race at Brands Hatch, Adam Wilcox went on to take the 2000 championship in his Nortel Networks-sponsored car, with Ed Horner second and Mark Cole third.

For 2001 there were few changes. The Sport Elise received further uprated

Adam Wilcox in his Nortel Networks-sponsored Sport Elise on his way to victory in the 2000 championship. (Lotus)

suspension and a dog-engagement gearbox, while the engine's cooling was improved and a programmable ECU was installed. To offer further pull for the drivers, the overall champion could win a drive in the final FIA Sportscar Championship race of the season at Kyalami, and the Rookie of the Year would be awarded a test in a Production Class British Touring Car with Barwell Motorsport. Otherwise the format was the same: 13 races supporting the BTCC and FIA Sports Car series and visiting Brands Hatch (twice), Thruxton, Silverstone (twice), Donington Park, Knockhill, Snetterton, Croft, Oulton Park, Mondello Park in Ireland, Spa-Francorchamps in Belgium and the Nürburgring in Germany. Among the new sponsors for 2001 was Carlube, with Lotus Motorsport lending its support to a new oil, Triple R, which was used in the Autobytel cars. It was the Carlube-liveried Elise that would end 2001 as champion, with driver Mark Fullalove taking six victories in his second season in the Autobytel championship. Always the bridesmaid, never the bride, Mark Cole improved one place from the previous year to take second.

The pack spreads out at Brands Hatch during a 2001 season race.
(Lotus)

Considering that the series was all about exposure for Lotus it was a relative success, and supporting such a high-profile series as the British Touring Car Championship was always going to pull the crowds. For the 2001 season there was extra coverage as *Autocar* road tester Chris Harris joined the fray. Despite lacklustre results, briefly flirting with the podium but with sixth his best finish, this was the first season of racing for Harris and his regular updates certainly increased public awareness of the championship.

In spite of the media coverage, support for the series waned during the 2001 season as sponsorship became harder to come by and costs mounted. Drivers were unhappy that they were paying some £65,000 for just 13 races, without even a car to show for it at the end of the year. As grids were depleted, cars were invited from the rival Club Lotus and Kelsport-sponsored series to create a B class and swell the grids. Although scheduled to run for three years, the Autobytel Lotus Championship was cancelled after its second season as part of the sweeping cost-cutting alterations from incoming chief executive Terry Playle.

But that was not the end of the story for Lotus Motorsport. From the outset, the Sport Elise had been intended for more than just the Autobytel championship and was available for privateers too. 'We wanted to sell customer race cars to be used around the world that could do anything from sprints and hill-climbs to 24-hour endurance racing,'

Mark Fullalove blazes a trail in the Carlube-sponsored Sport Elise en-route to the 2001 championship crown. (Lotus)

said Chris Arnold. Because the Sport Elise was equipped with a detachable front splitter and adjustable rear wing you could modify the car for low downforce or high downforce, depending where you raced, and if you didn't know, you just asked. 'There are a couple of race engineers based within the team that people can ring up for advice and also we run an after-sales service,' Arnold continued. 'So say you stuffed your car in practice on the first day you could ring up and we can despatch things to you.'

Privateer success

Sport Elise sales were very successful considering how specialised the market was. 'There are now [end of 2001] 61 Sport Elises racing around the world, and in motorsport terms it has been quite a big programme,' said Arnold. 'Our major markets are Japan, Australia and the UK. There is a championship in Japan, but in Europe people tend to enter them in different categories of races, for example a car did the Spa 24

Hours this year and five cars were in the Vallelunga Six Hours. There's probably something like 250 Elise pure race cars thrashing round circuits around the world.'

Ever since a couple of Elise Trofeos raced in the Vallelunga Six-Hour Silver Cup Endurance Race back in 1997, the Elise has been a regular sight at the Italian circuit. For 2001, six privateer drivers clubbed together to hire the team, as Arnold explained: 'We took two cars down, a team manager, chief mechanic, engineers, mechanics – pretty much a total arrive-and-drive package. Effectively that's the first time we've done that, they just jetted in, got in the cars, practised, raced and then went home again.' One of the five Elises entered for the 2001 race even managed to squeeze on to the podium in third spot, but Arnold knew the car's limitations in terms of outright wins. 'It's been a class winner, certainly in Europe,' he said, 'but in terms of overall events it's generally not, because we're in the featherweight class. We haven't got an engine

A trio of customer Sport Elises ready to be sent out to compete in race series around the world.
(Lotus)

putting out 500bhp so we aren't going to win the Spa 24 Hours outright. It's the perfect engine for the Elise because it matches the character. But you have to remember that it started out as a 1.4 and we've grown it to 1800 and taken it to 300bhp. We could get another 10hp on top of that, but it becomes a trade off between reliability and performance – and also cost, which becomes exponential. What you find for endurance is that if you knock a bit off the top end power you increase the mid-range torque and 24-hour reliability at the same time.' With the expiry of the Autobytel championship, the cars used in the series were all rebuilt before being sold off to be campaigned privately. Mark Fullalove's championship-winning car was among those converted to enduro specification with a 100-litre fuel tank.

As one door closes, another opens, and so it was for Lotus Motorsport. For 2002 the team shifted its focus to a trio of new projects. With some changes in the regulations, the Exige and Elise became

eligible for the FIA N-GT series so the team began planning the alterations needed to the car to make it competitive. There was also a pair of racers launched at the *Autosport* Show in January 2002, based on the Elise S2 (see Chapter 6): the Scholarship Elise and Sport 190. Like the Series 1 version, the Sport 190 was a pure track version available as an update to existing cars and eligible for both the Lotus Road Sport Series and the Intermarque Challenge of the AMOC. The package featured similar equipment to the S1, with the addition of Corbeau race seats and black alloy wheels wearing track-specification but road-legal Yokohama Advan AO48 tyres, and cost £10,587 at launch. The first customer Sport 190 was delivered to its Swiss owner in February of the same year.

Chris Arnold explained the theory behind the Elise Scholarship car: 'It's a safety kit really, covering you for MSA and basic FIA regulations.' Developed in conjunction with Safety Devices, the car was to be available as

With the Elise S2 came the possibility of a whole new generation of racing cars, first of which was to be the Scholarship Elise for racing virgins. (Lotus)

a kit of accessories or ready built, with Motorsport engineers fitting the necessary parts at critical moments on the production line. The specification included a five-point roll cage, competition seat and harness, fire extinguisher and electrical kill switches. The car was designed as part of a Scholarship package, much like the Caterham Academy scheme, which comprised a Caterham Seven car to keep, a test day, an ARDS course to obtain a racing licence, two hill-climbs, two sprints and four races, all for a very reasonable £14,950 including VAT. The Elise package was to include tuition and the ARDS course at the Hethel test track, with the opportunity to compete in two sprints, two hill-climbs and two circuit races.

Russell Carr's sketch for the outrageous Elise-based Lotus GT1. (Lotus)

GT1: an Elise too far?

The ultra-stiff Elise chassis could always handle more than the standard car's paltry 118bhp – but surely over 500bhp would be madness? Yet that is exactly what GTI Lotus Racing gave it when it shoehorned a V8 engine into the back of a modified Elise. 'It started with the Esprit,' recalled Lotus Motorsport general manager Chris Arnold. 'They went out to the 'States and did a lot of racing as they were having a big sales push on the Esprit. That morphed into the GT1 project, which has an Elise chassis stretched with a tubular frame to fit the V8 in longitudinally.'

The Esprit V8, unveiled at Geneva in 1996, provided an ideal basis for a GT car. The independent GTI Lotus Racing was formed, leasing part of Ketteringham Hall, the former home of Team Lotus, back from the Chapman family to develop the car for the FIA GT series. The Type 114 Esprit GT1 was the product, but for 1997 came an all-new,

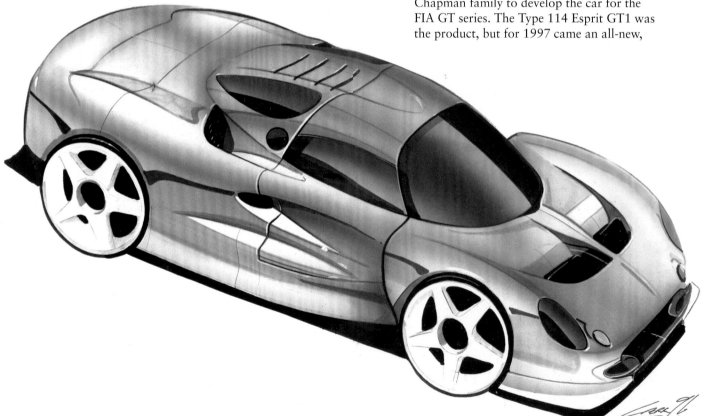

more aerodynamic Lotus GT1, Type 115, usually referred to as the Elise GT1 because of its grown-up Elise styling.

Like the Elise itself, the GT1 was developed in record time, with both road and race versions ready within eight months of its June 1996 inception, the project taking a skin-of-the-teeth approach reminiscent of the days of Colin Chapman and Team Lotus. Stylist Russell Carr designed this stunningly aggressive incarnation of the Elise, sculpting a new carbon-fibre body that looked like the offspring of a union between an Elise and a McLaren F1, yet remained recognisably related to the little Lotus road car, even using its windscreen and wiper. Despite being 769mm longer than the Elise, thanks to a wheelbase stretched by 375mm to accommodate the longitudinal V8, and 250mm wider, the GT1 was 102mm lower and just 177kg (390lb) heavier, hitting its 900kg (1,985lb) target weight. Developed with the aid of the wind tunnel, the GT1 was peppered with wings, diffusers and every available aerodynamic device to combine low drag with high downforce. There was a long tail covering the V8 engine, pronounced intakes aft of the front wheelarches and wing

mirrors mounted on stalks atop each arch, yet the overall shape remained both coherent and handsome.

Lotus Engineering's Richard Rackham, who was involved with the racing Esprits including the car that went to Le Mans in 1993, recalled the modifications needed to turn the Elise into a competitive GT car. 'There is substantial stiffening because although the Elise chassis is stiff enough for a little road car, for a GT car it wasn't, so a steel roll cage was bolted on top. There were various modifications to the suspension pickup points to take a beefier system with transversely mounted spring/damper units, with other modifications around the fuel tank area to give greater fuel capacity.'

Vast, 18in five-spoke Speedline magnesium alloy wheels filled the arches, hiding equally massive 14in disc brakes, in either cast iron or carbon, with six-pot AP Racing calipers. And they were needed. When fitted with a pair of Allied Signal turbochargers the fuel-injected 3,506cc 32-valve V8 put some 550bhp through the GT1's Hewland six-speed sequential gearbox; that's more than 610bhp/tonne. Living up to the Lotus reputation for innovation, and further

The completed GT1 clay shows what a large machine it had become. (Lotus)

The unique Lotus GT1 road car at the Lotus Festival 2002, following an extensive refit. (James Elliott)

proving the versatility of the aluminium chassis, its extruded construction allowed the hollow main side members to double as cooling ducts, piping cold air from the front of the car directly to the rear brakes. The solid suspension was fully rose-jointed and benefited from lightweight dampers and racing springs.

Rackham was part of a team of Lotus engineers sent to Ketteringham Hall to create a roadgoing version of the GT1 to homologate the racer, creating at the same time the ultimate Elise road car. A detuned 350bhp version of the 3,506cc V8 was used to make the car a bit less wild and gone were the racer's built-in air jacks and huge rear wing. Fortunately, the efficiency of the standard Elise crash structure helped Lotus persuade the powers that be it would be easily sufficient for the new model's 900kg, but the road car did need a handbrake and more conventional door mirrors. To give some semblance of suspension travel and bring the headlights up to a legal level the ride height was increased, while to comply with noise regulations the car acquired

additional silencers and a conventional Esprit gearbox. With nearly 390bhp/tonne the GT1 would have made a spectacular road car, but with its racing clutch it was virtually undriveable. Despite talk of a limited production run, the car was unfortunately never developed properly, as Rackham recalled: 'It was never a serious road car, it was a homologation special – very powerful, but unsorted. We went round the track to check the systems before it went off for testing and it wasn't terribly pleasant, it was very noisy because it was just a carbon fibre shell.' Having been finished just in time for the homologation deadline, the sole road car was eventually auctioned – still finished in bare carbon-fibre – by owner GTI. It was then lost in the ether for a while, before being tracked down by Club Lotus and displayed at its Lotus Festival 2002. Now totally re-engineered, the car had been painted and wore badges proclaiming it as 'Elise GT1'. The original twin-turbo V8 had been reinstated with the Hewland six-speed sequential gearbox, and it now boasted a terrifying 575bhp and 420lb ft (569.5Nm) of

The Elise GT1 holds off the chasing pack at the Nürburgring. (LAT)

torque. Inside, the GT1 was familiarly Elise, even down to the standard pedals, but oppressively dark and unusually plush, with properly padded seats, CD player and a beautifully detailed gearlever that was almost sculpture. One other car, one of the racers, also made its way on to the road thanks to owner and former GTI Racing boss Toine Hezemans, who made his GT1 road-legal for the 2001 Supercar Rally.

Completed and homologated, the GT1 proved quick in testing when compared with the preceding Esprit and rivals from McLaren and Porsche, so all the building blocks were in place for further Lotus track success. But as Rackham explained, the carpet was whipped out from under the GT1's wheels. 'The car would have been very competitive because at the time you could have a turbo engine with a certain restrictor size or a non-turbo engine with a big restrictor to restrict air into the engine. This would have given the GTI team an advantage. A few weeks before the beginning of the season the regulations changed, so suddenly it was uncompetitive. People like Porsche were able to just pick an

engine off the shelf.' With some butchery of the neat engine bay, the bulkier, Lotus-designed 6.0-litre Corvette LT5 V8 engine fitted and was hurriedly developed in time for the start of the season. Three cars ran with the new engine, but it was both thirsty, requiring extra fuel stops, and under-developed, the team working on a budget that was a fraction of other 'works' teams. Then, part way through the season, the regulation changes were reversed after complaints to the FIA, but the GT1s struggled to find consistency. Group Lotus and GTI Racing Ltd split in late 1997 as Lotus decided it didn't want to spend any more money flogging a dead horse. GTI and two privateer teams continued with the Type 115, but lack of sponsorship eventually saw their efforts peter out, and the car's potential was never fully realised.

With a total of just seven racers built, the GT1 may have ended up a costly white elephant, but it showed just how far the Elise concept could be taken, with a fully fledged GT car incredibly based around the same basic chassis tub.

5 **Variations** on a theme

For most, the standard Lotus Elise is as extreme a car as they will ever want or need. But for the select few it simply isn't enough, and when road testers from *Autocar* magazine suggested to Lotus engineers that a more raw version would be well received, the result was the stunning 340R.

Although based on a standard chassis, the new car had to be very different to avoid treading on the Elise's toes and it became a much more radical incarnation, pared to the minimum and reviving some of the simplicity of the first 'step-in' concepts. It also took the Elise nearer to the design and engineering purity of the Ducati superbikes that had inspired the M111 project team, becoming resolutely minimal in all but price, which was to be substantially higher than a standard car.

'We always had the idea to do a car without a body on it,' explained Julian Thomson. 'We felt there may be a demand from Lotus Seven people to do a very minimal separate-fendered car, which is basically what 340R was.' Taking a theme that began with the Elise Sprint (see Chapter 3) the 340R blew it out of all proportion, with a target weight of just 500kg (1,100lb) and a target power-to-weight ratio of

The preferred design for the spectacular Lotus 340R was that of incoming head of design, Russell Carr. (Lotus)

340bhp/tonne, which, when the 'R' from the lightweight 26R racing Elan was added, gave the car its name. The designers had wanted it to run without a windscreen, considering a 'fresh air screen' as featured on the Sprint, but a ride in the now road-legal concept car was enough to persuade Thomson and stylist Russell Carr against the plan. Codenamed 'Enid', up to 400-500 340Rs per year were considered, although in the end it remained a limited-run special edition, largely penned by Carr assisted by Steven Crijns, with the interior by Matt Hill.

With the basic style resolved on paper, a written-off Elise chassis was used as the basis of the first clay, before a running prototype was constructed with all-new components for the 340R's show debut, the 1998 Birmingham Motor Show at the National Exhibition Centre. 'It was fun because it was no compromise and a very quick turnaround,' recalled Carr, 'The show car took 16 weeks from first sketch to pushing the car on to the stand.' And it certainly wowed the crowds, with wild looks that were more like a Dan Dare spacecraft than the friendly Elise. The stiffness of the extruded and bonded chassis allowed the bodywork to remain minimal as it is not part of the car's structure and a composite one-

A number of cues from the design by stylist Steven Crijns were also integrated into the final form of 340R. (Lotus)

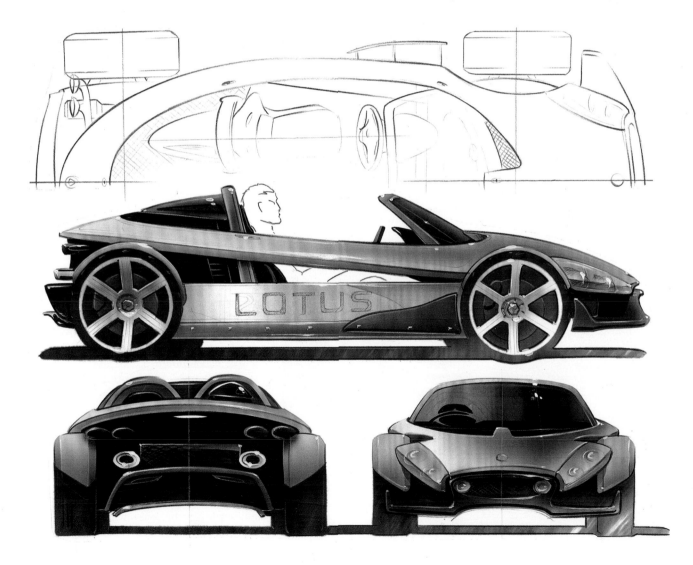

The crowds at the 1998 British Motor Show at the Birmingham NEC were wowed by the unveiling of the 340R. (Lotus)

An exhaust system by motorcycle specialist Motad adorned the tail of the 340R show car. (Lotus)

piece removable body was formed, leaving the wheels open with only lightweight cycle wings that could be removed for track use. Exposing more of the elegant chassis, the body gave the 340R the look of a double-width single-seater racing car, but with a hint of beach buggy about the chubby tail with its exposed K-series engine. There were distinctive 'point-source' headlamps fared into slashes down the nose for improved aerodynamics and an aggressive look, with the rear lights mounted on stalks. Removable panels gave access for checking the levels, and there were translucent panels in the gaps in the sides to let the driver sense the road rushing by his elbow. The OZ Racing alloy wheels were shod with hand-cut Yokohama tyres and the motorbike theme was enhanced by an exposed exhaust created by bike specialist Motad.

With no doors, driver and passenger clambered over the cockpit sides and into lightweight, Alcantara-trimmed composite

The 340R show car interior was every bit as radical as the exterior, complete with starter button and individually cowled instruments. (Lotus)

racing seats with four-point competition harnesses by Safety Devices. There was a cut-down Elise screen ahead, and behind, further stiffening the chassis, sat a pair of stylish interlocking 'Speedster bars' developed by Safety Devices to offer protection after the removal of the standard Elise roll hoop. The dashboard was replaced with swooping aluminium cross-pieces, with a central brace housing the switchgear and topped with a starter button. Motorcycle-style separate Stack rev counter and speedometer sat ahead of the quick-release Momo steering wheel.

Although initially unveiled as a concept car, the fantastic reaction the 340R received at the NEC persuaded Lotus to announce at Geneva in March 1999 that it would be built, and the production-ready car was at the Earls Court show just seven months later. There were changes to meet European type approval, but enthusiasts who paid their deposits on seeing the concept car would not be disappointed with a watered-down production car, for the roadgoing 340R still managed to make the Elise look boring. There were no special colour schemes, all cars being finished in the same titanium and black as the show car, although there was a larger grille with integral driving lamps and bigger mudguards. A Formula One-style two-blade wing was fitted on the nose to counteract the front-end lift found in wind tunnel tests, and a spoiler was added to the rear as part of a tail restyle including a legally required engine cover, a Janspeed exhaust, and a high-level brake light. The windscreen was extended and elegant wing mirrors by Aprilia were fitted on each side. Inside, a standard gearknob replaced the stylish but uncomfortable show version and there was a conventional steering wheel, with the quick-release item retained as a track option. There were no niceties such as a stereo, windows or even a roof, making it very much a summer car, although there was a basic tonneau cover.

Exposed!
The ultimate
Elise

Maybe the 340R is not fast enough; too heavy; too civilised. If so, Exposé is the answer, a unique track-only prototype built at the behest of product manager Tony Shute as a serious contender for the Scratch Award in the Paul Matty Lotus Hillclimb Championship. 'For me it was unfinished business,' said Shute. 'I wasn't involved in 340R and I really wanted to build the ultimate Elise.'

With Shute's obsession with light weight, it was inevitable that the Exposé would be scantily clad, so windscreen, passenger seat, heater, mudguards, handbrake, lights and half the roll bar all fell by the wayside. But the biggest difference came from the all-new body. 'The idea came from my son,' Shute explained. 'He was racing a 1/10th scale radio-controlled Lotus GT1 made from polycarbonate and I was hill-climbing a 340R. His idea was: 'Why don't you take the body off my car and stick it on the 340R and you might win'. So we got Lotus to back it, they built the car and it was really

successful, it's got five class records.'

In September 2000, Lotus donated a track-pack 340R as a guinea pig and permitted a minimal budget (reportedly less than £35,000) to develop the car, and by January 2001 Exposé was ready to roll. The polycarbonate body, a similar material to that used for police riot shields, was created by vacuum forming four panels from 3-4mm thick sheets, and with its transparent finish it allows you to see the guts of the 340R, and its elegant extruded chassis, in all their glory. It also halves the weight of the body to just 25kg (55lb), making the total weight of Exposé some 130kg (287lb) less than a 'standard' road 340R. Much like the remote-controlled car that inspired it, the Exposé's body is located by pins and circlips, with the addition of industrial Velcro to prevent it flapping around.

The weight saving translates to scintillating performance, with an estimated 0-60mph in just 3.5 seconds and a top speed of 140mph (225km/h). With the addition of adjustable dampers and race springs from the Sport Elise, and wide slick tyres (16in front, 17in rear), the Exposé is a serious tool. 'With lightweight wheels its kerb weight is 545kg (1,200lb) and it's got 190hp, it's a very useful bit of kit' said Shute. 'What I'd like to do is get another 50

kilos out of it, there is still some to go. The other cars that compete in the series, mainly old Lotus Formula 2 and Formula 3 cars, are still much lighter, but the chassis is so good and the traction, particularly in the wet, is outstanding. It's about nine seconds to 100mph so it's a very fun car to drive.' Not only performance was boosted by the Shute Slim-Fast plan, the reduction of weight also sharpened the other responses of the already cut-throat 340R. 'I'm a great believer in performance through light weight,' said Shute, 'but it wasn't until we got Exposé running that I realised just how fantastic it was, not really in straight line speed but all the other benefits: the braking, the cornering. Just by getting 10 per cent of the weight out, the benefits are really quite different to just sticking a more powerful engine in.'

Fun it may be, but the Exposé is not just a toy. The concept demonstrates the talents of Lotus Engineering with a material that could be a realistic possibility for production cars one day. Not only is it light and cheap, but it is easy to tool, recyclable and strong without being brittle. Properly resolved, it could lead companies to offer interchangeable bodies with integral bumpers, and in its transparent form you can even shine the headlights through the body.

Changes under the skin were extensive, but not as revolutionary as anticipated. 'There wasn't too much we could change because of the volume of the cars,' explained vehicle dynamics engineer Matt Becker. 'The tyres were developed for the 190 Sport so we knew their performance was good, especially in dry conditions. The spring rates were identical to the 190 Sport, but because the car was lighter it was naturally a bit more responsive. The rear anti-roll bar was about the only thing we changed, and the suspension geometry was slightly different.' While the show car remained basically as a standard Elise, down to its 118bhp K-series, the 340R justified its price tag with a unit tuned to produce 177bhp at 7,800rpm in roadgoing trim, with a 'track pack' version also offered with a sports exhaust and a huge 190bhp. The suspension featured adjustable

platform Koni dampers, the stiff set-up sacrificing some ride quality in return for more responsive handling. There was awesome grip from the Yokohama AO38 LTS (Lotus) semi-slick tyres, and there was the same superb Elise steering rack. Cross-drilled ventilated discs with AP Racing calipers provided ample stopping power, and although a planned right-hand race-style gearchange never made it past the drawing board, there was a close-ratio gearbox to exploit the rev-happy engine.

Unfortunately, the car was much heavier on the road than planned and fell well short of its target power-to-weight ratio. The 675kg (1,488lb) road car achieved just 262bhp/tonne, so the 340 tag was converted to a reference to the total production volume. But it was still comfortably the quickest Elise road variant so far, both in a straight line

Tony Shute's stripped-out, transparent polycarbonate-bodied Exposé at rest. (Lotus)

The Exposé attacks the Shelsley Walsh hill-climb in 2001 with Tony Shute at the wheel. (Paul Hardiman)

The production-ready 340R looks more at home here at Brands Hatch than on the road. (Lotus)

and around a track, with awesome handling that virtually eradicated understeer and oversteer in normal conditions. Cycle wings made the 340R easy to position on the road and it offered instant throttle response, with additional inlet valving that opened as the revs rose to boost power and noise. Unfettered by bodywork, the engine noise was given full cry, but testers noted a tendency for heat soak in the footwells caused by the radiators that could become almost unbearable on the track.

Making a thrilling road car or a staggeringly fast track day tool, all 340 cars sold quickly after going on sale in December 1999, despite a hefty £35,000 price tag.

Although there was some criticism of it missing its target weight by some distance, the 340R was praised by the press. *Autocar* road tester Steve Sutcliffe enthused: 'Quite extraordinary. I never thought I'd drive a road car in which you could carry more speed into corners than you can in a Caterham 7, but the 340R is it.' *Road & Track* called it: 'Simply the purest driving machine on the planet.'

Race car for the road

But the 340R was never intended as anything more than a toy for roofless summer fun and weekend track visits. For those who wanted thrills, drama and track day fun all year

Matt Becker shakes down the 340R show car at Hethel. Unlike production versions, the show car was powered by a standard 118bhp Elise unit. (Lotus)

Extra power and even less weight made the 340R blindingly quick, although it still lagged behind the projected power-to-weight of 340bhp/tonne. (Virgin Interactive)

round, the answer was unveiled in early 2000, the awesome Exige. When the Autobytel Lotus Championship began, Lotus press releases claimed that the Sport Elise would not become a road car, yet Exige was the literal example of motorsport improvements returning to the road. 'We came back after Christmas having decided not to do the car,' recalled incoming head of design Russell Carr, 'then in the second week in January someone came up and said: 'We want it to be at Geneva this year'. We had until the end of February to turn it into a show car.' For practicality, the Exige does not have a removable rear clamshell, and the tailgate is hinged and transparent, but otherwise it remains very close to the racer. Lotus Motorsport general manager Chris Arnold explained: 'There is a crossover and the Exige is the extreme example, we literally lifted the whole race bodywork and transferred it back on to a road car. Body-wise it's pretty much identical apart from the more stylised rear wing and low-downforce front splitter.'

'Exige just took the game forward,' remarked evaluation engineer Alastair McQueen, 'it was more of a road car than the 340. I think a lot of people bought a 340R because of the way it looks. Whereas I think most people bought the Exige for the way it drives.' That's not to say it didn't look fantastic. If there was a criticism to level at the styling of the Elise, it's that it was perhaps a little too friendly, not as aggressive as it could be. The Exige quashes any such thoughts with a squat stance and traffic-halting looks that are enough to make a petrolhead weak at the knees. Unlike the 340R, the Exige was a built-to-order production model rather than a special edition, and a relative bargain at £29,995 with the same 177bhp version of the K-series engine, although most buyers opted for the additional £900 sports exhaust and 190bhp VHPD option. 'When we did the business plans we saw a limited run of road replicas,' Arnold explained, 'but we were so pleased with the styling that we went beyond what I had originally envisaged.'

A true racer for the road, the Exige looks like a carbon copy of the Sport Elise race car, as this design sketch shows.
(Lotus)

The Exige provides one of the most intense driving experiences around, and with the aerodynamic tweaks and wider tyres the car feels nailed to the road. (Tony Baker)

Extra vents and ducts scoop air in to cool vital areas in the engine bay, such as the alternator. (Tony Baker)

Although its price was aimed squarely at the Audi TT and Porsche Boxster marketplace, the Exige was always a much more focused machine thanks to its racer genes and would only ever be bought by driving purists, avoiding the poseurs' market that the Elise is – just – soft enough to tempt. Like the 340R, much of the Exige specification is similar to that of the Sport 190, but the fixed-head car drifts even nearer to the Sport Elise, Lotus even having briefly considered retaining its central seating position. 'The engine is also a detuned version of the race engine,' explained Arnold, 'but in terms of suspension and brakes you drift back more towards the road car. We didn't bring over the suspension dampers, but they are available. Some things you do on the track you can't do on the road, but there is a history of parts that were developed for the race car that have become available, we can even do you a complete carbon-fibre Exige if you want.'

Sitting on the road the Exige – derived from *exiger*, French for demand – dares you to drive it with its baby Group C sports prototype looks, a feast of intakes and wings. And feeding yourself between the wide sill and the tight roof only serves to heighten the experience, turning every shopping trip into a mini Le Mans. Once inside, there is the familiar driving position and to make it even more the road racer, options included competition seats with full harnesses and a removable steering wheel. The enclosed cabin was gloomy, with only extra Alcantara panels on the dashboard to liven things up a bit, and there was no standard radio, although like the Elise, an aerial is provided, but mounted on the roof rather than the engine cover. The Exige took impracticality to new lows, the leather stowage flaps either side of the gearlever were gone, it had a roof yet could still leak in a downpour, and there was no boot to speak of, only an unprotected shelf behind the airbox to ensure your frozen goods were thoroughly defrosted within five miles of the supermarket. Reversing was made near impossible by the restrictive harnesses specified on most cars and by the

polycarbonate engine cover which gave outsiders a good look at the car's powerplant, but was too cloudy to give the driver any kind of rearward vision.

But talk of practicality is irrelevant when considering the Exige, and it is only when you fire up the engine that you start to see the point. Get past the standard alarm and immobiliser, turn the key and there is a frantic whirring followed by a chuntering clatter as the K-series turns over. Then it sounds like the hounds of hell have hopped in for the ride, with just a small screen separating the engine from the driver's ears; the amplified buzz-saw sound filling the cabin is spectacular. Once you get used to its hunting idle and the VHPD engine's cammy nature it feels much like an Elise, but more honed than any of its other high-performance variants and with beefier, confidence-inspiring steering. A weight disadvantage means that the Exige lags behind the 340R in acceleration, but it makes up for it with drama. To keep the engine singing you have to stir that close-ratio gearbox to keep the revs between the 5,000rpm and the peak power delivery at 7,800rpm, with the rev limiter cutting in just 200rpm later. The little K-series screams away just millimetres behind driver's ears and the thumps and squeaks from the suspension add to the aural assault, but it is not without its rewards.

The performance is incredibly accessible, the family trait of excellent ride and handling compromise meaning the car is not put off by poor surfaces. The aggressive styling isn't all for show; the roof scoop cools the alternator and the aerodynamic aids, such as the front splitter, rear wing and Kamm tail, add 80kg (176lb) of extra downforce at 100mph (161km/h) making its attraction for the road magnetic. The brakes, cross-drilled discs with two-piston AP front calipers and single-pot Brembo rears, as on the 340R, are simply astounding once warm. Pumped-up wheelarches cover the same wider track and alloy wheels as the Sport Elise, shod with Yokohama A039 tyres, 195s up front with sticky 225 rears. Dry grip is simply massive, with none of the standard car's tendency to understeer, so how fast you corner is more down to how brave you are. A fantastically stiff suspension set-up means there is virtually no body roll. When it rains, things get a little more tricky and power needs to be fed in with some care to avoid swapping ends, and when the limits are reached, you need to be a hero to catch an Exige, for it snaps more violently than the standard car, or even the 340R.

Probably the best Elise variant for the track, the Exige unfortunately meant compromising on the road as it made a tiring motorway car and the engine's cammy nature made it wearing around town. 'Initially, the Exige wasn't too successful, then all of a sudden it took off,' noted Matt Becker. 'On circuit days you see so many Exiges, they are quick on a circuit with the 190 engine and the different gear ratios – the amount of grip they generate from

Perhaps not the most outrageous Elise variant, but the stunning Exige is certainly the most desirable. (Tony Baker)

The pronounced front splitter and rear wing are not just for show, providing 80kg (176lb) of extra downforce at 100mph (161km/h). (Tony Baker)

Fabulous matt-black alloy wheels as found on the Sport Elise racer look absolutely superb. (Tony Baker)

downforce is just mindblowing.' On the open road, the Exige was one of the most intense driving experiences possible. It may not have had the straight-line speed of a supercar, but it was every bit as involving and had the chassis dynamics and incredible grip to help it corner as well, if not better. As *Autocar* road tester Steve Sutcliffe put it: 'The Exige is so stimulating dynamically that you often have to tell yourself to calm down a little when you're driving it, in order not to get too carried away.' Colleague Chris Harris ran one as a long-term test car for a year, while also competing in the Autobytel championship, and discovered both the joy and pain of owning an Exige. The car was used as a daily driver and thrashed around track days at the weekends, covering a substantial mileage. But it suffered serial unreliability, an alarming thirst for oil culminating in an engine failure after just 5,800 miles.

Inside as out, the Exige looks, sounds and feels every inch the scaled-down Group C racing car. (Tony Baker)

Unfortunately, incoming emissions regulations meant the last Exige was built before the end of 2001, but it remains a dramatic and memorable Elise variation. Vehicle dynamics engineer Gavan Kershaw explained the pros and cons of the Exige and 340R: 'They're good cars for what they do, but they only do one job. They are very fast track cars and you take a lot of other bits to have that performance. And I think the Elise in its raw state is good enough for everything, if you want to go for a quick drive on a track day or if you want to go on holiday, it does all of those things. The trouble comes when you try to seek the last little bit. If you got 10 per cent more handling out of the Elise, you'd probably lose 30 per cent of the ride. You catch it out and get on a certain type of road and the thing starts to act a bit like a pogo stick because it's got high spring rates. I've never driven an Elise in any circumstances where I'm unhappy with something or frustrated by it.' That sounds like criticism, but Kershaw sums up the Exige appeal with ease: 'Say you do Knockhill track day and you've got eight hours in an Exige, driving mainly motorways. You get there, you're tired and you think "why do I bother?" Then three laps in you wouldn't swap it for the world.'

Lotus by another name

Versatility is a word that continues to reappear when referring to Richard Rackham's innovative Elise chassis design and it was a feature that was to rear its head again at the Geneva Motor Show in March 1999. On the Opel stand sat a dynamic new two-seat roadster, with angular and aggressive styling by General Motors's design director Martin Smith and with remarkably similar dimensions to the Lotus Elise. The reason soon became clear. The Opel

Taking
over the
asylum

Not since McLaren designer Gordon Murray's wonderfully barking Rocket of the early 1990s had there been such a beautifully executed but logic-defying road car as the 340R. But as it hit the road, the Lotus found plenty of rivals to give it a run for its money.

Like the 340R, the Strathcarron SC-5A was designed as an extreme version of a mid-engined Elise-style concept, even using an Elise screen. Conceived back in 1994, the production car arrived at the 2000 Birmingham Motor Show, keenly priced at £22,450. Engineered by Reynard and built in Norfolk by Chapman Associates, it was powered by a 125bhp 1,180cc Triumph motorcycle engine with six-speed sequential gearbox and de Dion rear suspension. Thanks to a composite tub it weighed just 550kg (1,213lb) and sparkling performance encouraged buyers, but unfortunately just 11 production cars were built. Also appearing at Birmingham in 2000 were the Ginetta G20 and Grinnall IV. At £13,000 the retro-style road-racer Ginetta was cheap, but build quality and handling were leagues below the Lotus, as was performance despite 138bhp 1,796cc Ford Zetec power. The four-wheeled successor to the loopy Grinnall III had potential, with 235bhp Fiat turbo power, under 600kg (1,323lb) and a sub-£25,000 projected price. But the car was still far from production-ready by the time the last 340R hit the streets.

Probably the 340R's keenest rival came from Caterham Cars. Its Seven dates back to 1958, but by the turn of the millennium had evolved into the road missile Superlight R500. A frankly silly incarnation of perhaps the world's least practical car, it boasted 500bhp per tonne and a breathtaking 0-60mph of 3.4 seconds. At £32,000 it was competitive on price and featured the classic Seven telepathic steering, awesome brakes and grip and a six-speed gearbox. While looking at Caterham, it's worth mentioning the other Seven-based rivals, the more competent of which included the Dax Rush, available with V8, Cosworth and 'bike engines, and the simply ridiculous Westfield Megabusa. Powered by the 1,300cc Suzuki Hayabusa motorcycle unit, this rev-hungry screamer boasted 180bhp at 9,800rpm, weighed just 440kg (970lb) and went from 0-60mph in less than four seconds, all for £22,000.

Although it may not look it, the closest in philosophy to the 340R was Simon Saunders's Ariel Atom. This was another example of a Seven for the millennium, originally to use the Triumph motorbike engine as the Strathcarron, but finally opting for the same mid-mounted 1.8 K-series as the Elise and 340R. Power options ranged from 125bhp to 195bhp, with prices from £16,000 to well over £30,000 to suit. The cycle-winged Atom was a no-compromise fun car, minimal bodywork dropping its weight to below 500kg (1,100lb) with the trellis chassis fully visible. Revealed in early 1999, the car was on the road by October and offered awesome yet affordable performance and handling.

For the Exige, the obvious rivals are somewhat harder to come by. You can look at the same cars that might have tempted buyers away from the 340R, and the attraction of the Exige lies in the bonus of a roof on wet track days. But in some ways it was a more mainstream offering and, although undoubtedly raw, more usable than the toy-like 340R. In essence, and in price at least, the Exige was a car to tempt buyers away from softer £30,000 sports cars, offering the performance to match – and the looks and handling to beat – the Porsche Boxster, Audi TT and BMW Z3 3.0-litre. Honda's Integra R was cheaper and provided the same kind of frenetic thrills, thanks to a 2.0-litre engine that produced its 218bhp maximum at a heady 8,000rpm, giving it a 0-60mph time of 6.5 seconds. For anything to come remotely close to the drama of the Exige, it's back to Blighty. Similarly wild, although substantially faster and costlier, is TVR's Tuscan Speed Six, but it is much more a bruising poseur's sports car than racer for the road. The nearest rival to the Exige was the Noble M12, developed from the ugly Elise-rival M10 roadster. Produced by the tiny Noble Moy Automotive team in Leicestershire, the M12 looked good, although with an awkwardness you won't find in the stunning baby Group C racer looks of the Exige. But on the road the Noble was a true supercar, with performance that comfortably eclipsed the Exige, thanks to 316bhp/tonne, despite being more than 200kg (440lb) heavier at 980kg (2,161lb). Like the Exige, it used a mass-produced power unit, in this case the 2,595cc Ford Duratec V6, but with two Garrett T25 turbochargers it propelled the M12 to 60mph in 3.9 seconds and on to 155mph (250km/h). Launched at the Birmingham Motor Show in 2000, the Noble had many parallels with the Exige, with a superb chassis, huge grip, five-speed gearbox and cross-drilled and ventilated discs without ABS. But the Exige's trump card was a bank manager-pleasing price tag that undercut the still reasonable £44,950 Noble by more then £10,000.

Speedster was a collaboration between GM and Lotus, mating a modified version of the extruded and bonded Elise chassis to the Astra Coupé's all-aluminium 2,198cc 16-valve Ecotec 'four' in an effort to boost the brand appeal of GM's staid Opel and Vauxhall marques. 'We've worked with them before and in effect they wanted a piece of Lotus,' explained Gavan Kershaw, who worked with the engineers from Vauxhall in developing the car, tagged VX220 in the UK. 'They can't understand why people buy Lotuses, but they realised that it was exactly what their brand needed. They needed a sports car, for Germany especially, to give the brand some hype.'

With 500bhp per tonne and telepathic steering, the Caterham R500 is spectacularly fast on road or track. (Tony Baker)

Although faster than the Exige and equal to the Lotus in handling, the Noble M12 GTO lacked its stunning looks and sublime steering feel, and cost substantially more. (Noble)

There was also assistance from Lotus Design to productionise the GM concept and at the 1999 Earls Court Motor Show, Lotus announced that they would build 2,000 Opel Speedsters and 1,000 Vauxhall VX220s annually at Hethel. 'We were making Elises on quite a small production line,' said Kershaw, 'Then someone sat down and said 'we want to build 3,000 of these things as well', which means we've got to build a whole new factory with a capability of building 6-10,000 cars per year.' Given the codename Skipton by the factory, the GM car was far more than just an Elise with a makeover, as Kershaw explained: 'We're looking at 10 per cent carry-over

GM Design Director Martin Smith penned sharp new lines for the Elise-based Opel Speedster/Vauxhall VX220. (Vauxhall)

components between the two: fixings, radiators, indicator stalks and stuff like that. And that's fine because it doesn't interfere with how the car drives, it's got a different interior and it drives differently.'

Although based on an Elise tub, with the sills cut down by 50mm for easier access, the Vauxhall boasted a longer wheelbase, a wider track, particularly at the rear to accommodate the beefier new motor, and larger overall dimensions meaning it was never likely to be quite as agile. It was also substantially heavier at 875kg (1,929lb), but there was superbly direct steering and a similar double wishbone set-up giving the expected excellent ride/handling compromise, if a little softer. But with new Bilstein dampers, wider rear track and the skinny 175-section front tyres adorning those hefty 17in alloys, there was the safe mild understeer expected of a Vauxhall model. A standard servo and anti-lock system were sensible additions to the brakes, boosting both comfort and safety. However, the new car's trump card was its engine, with a useful 145bhp at 5,800rpm and a massive – in Elise terms – 150lb ft (203Nm) of torque at 4,000rpm from a totally unstressed unit. Power was delivered via a slick Getrag five-speed gearbox, but despite the extra grunt the

Vauxhall's weight meant both its economy and performance lagged behind its Lotus sibling, with 0-60mph reached in 6.1 seconds, although the extra torque boosted top speed to 132mph (212km/h).

The Lotus ride and handling engineers, assisting representatives from Vauxhall, were able to ensure that the VX220 behaved differently enough to the Elise to ensure there was a marketplace for both cars. 'There was a reasonable amount of input from Lotus Engineering,' Kershaw admitted, 'they've set their car up for the way they want an Opel or a Vauxhall to drive. I don't think they wanted an Elise, they've got a totally different customer range to us.' Kershaw rates the Elise and VX220 as horses for courses: 'In certain circumstances and on certain days of the week I do enjoy how the VX drives. It is a typical large-capacity, very torquey unit and there are days of the week when everyone cries out for a car like that. And then other times, when you get to blast around a B-road or a track, you want to be at maximum rpm.'

The GM car's sharp-suited glassfibre body has a bulkier look with some great details such as the neat rear lights or the up-and-over tailpipes, but the Elise bloodline remains obvious, with innovative details including making the exhaust silencer part of the rear crash structure. The Vauxhall VX220 was a little less attractive to buyers than the near-identical Opel Speedster, thanks to an uninspiring name and less pleasing grille and badging.

But it was inside that a VX might have tempted potential Elise buyers away from a Lotus showroom and into a Vauxhall one. There was more comfort, a few more toys – it was a bit more Vauxhall. There was still lots of exposed aluminium, including a stylish optional extruded aluminium brace bar, but there was a conventional dashboard, albeit with a set of Stack instruments and a starter button mounted in the centre. In addition to the cut-down sills, longer doors aided entry and exit, although it was still not the most graceful operation, and there was sound deadening injected into the body cavities to add refinement. The driving position would

be familiar to Elise owners, but gone were Richard Rackham's lovely extruded pedals, although their drilled replacements were not unattractive, and ahead sat a tiny Momo wheel, the smallest ever to come complete with airbag. To add a bit of practicality there was a more user-friendly and watertight hood and a bigger boot. And the price for this extra power and comfort? Just £320 more than a basic Elise with a launch price tag of £22,995, plus £1,200 for a stylish optional hardtop.

The VX220 suffered from something of an image problem, in the UK at least, seen as a poor relation to the Lotus that sired it, a dilution of the purity of the original, or worse, a cynical cashing-in on the Elise success. It was a situation that wasn't helped by Vauxhall launching the car with a disastrous advertising campaign featuring comedian

The Vauxhall Griffin badging found on the VX220's grille lacks Lotus cachet, or even that of its Opel sibling. (Vauxhall)

The Vauxhall offers a more conventional and more luxurious interior than the Elise, but still remains spartan. (Vauxhall)

From this angle the VX220 is stylish and aggressive, and its neat new roof style is both handsome and watertight. (Vauxhall)

Griff Rhys-Jones clad in ginger beard, vest and Y-fronts to explain that the VX was the sexiest Vauxhall ever built. Cheap images of it toddling round the military test track at Chobham, Surrey, and Rhys-Jones's irritating

voice-overs did little to endear the new model to an already sceptical buying public. The press acclaimed the new car however, praising its mixture of friendlier Elise handling, torquey engine and improved interior, with *What Car?* presenting the Vauxhall with 'Best Roadster' in its Car of the Year Awards for both 2001 and 2002.

Channel 4's *Driven* television programme pitted a VX220 against its blood brother when the Elise Series 2 arrived (see Chapter 6) and found the Vauxhall the more practical car with a bigger boot and an easier and more leak-resistant hood. Former rally ace Penny Mallory commented: 'Inside it's got a lot more creature comforts, and of course that lovely 2.2-litre Vauxhall engine.' Mallory raised a point that a lot of enthusiasts will undoubtedly have asked themselves: 'It's so similar to the Elise it could have been cloned, it does make you wonder if Lotus haven't shot themselves in the foot by selling some of their best trade secrets to a direct competitor.' *Driven* found the Vauxhall to be brilliant fun to drive and controllable

To boost ailing VX220 sales in the UK, Vauxhall launched the dramatic Lightning Yellow special edition with unique yellow hardtop and mean black alloy wheels. (Vauxhall)

on the limit, but Mallory highlighted the car's biggest disability: 'Ultimately, a Lotus badge is going to have a bit more pull.'

This was confirmed in the showrooms. In 2001, Vauxhall shifted just 450 cars, little over half the projected target, although it was not aided by early production problems at Hethel. To try to boost sales, Vauxhall offered 0 per cent finance for the first three months of 2002 and launched a limited edition run of 100 aggressive-looking 'Lightning Yellow' VX220s. For an extra £2,000, each car bore bright yellow paint and matching hardtop, anthracite alloy wheels and a black windscreen surround, while inside were black leather seats, a CD player and a build number on the dashboard. Also announced in 2002, and due the following year, was the much-anticipated VX220 Turbo. A 178bhp Vectra V6 engine was considered, but it was heavy and the Astra Coupé's 2.0-litre turbo offered 187bhp and a whopping 184lb ft (249.5nm) of torque, giving it the potential to be one of best Elise-based cars yet. The model was

delayed by problems with heat dissipation in the engine bay, but once resolved it promised 0-60mph in well under five seconds, with a target price of £25,000.

Like Lotus, Vauxhall offered an 'Advanced Driver Training' scheme, although for VX220 customers it was free. Held at and developed in conjunction with Jonathan Palmer's PalmerSport school at Bedford Autodrome, the day involved tuition on road driving, handling and skid control, with the aid of on-board cameras and data logging systems. To suggest the VX220's potential as a track day car, Vauxhall also built a Sprint version in mid-2002, using mainly off-the-shelf Lotus Motorsport items such as Sport Elise adjustable suspension, and black Exige wheels. A revised version of the standard engine gave 165bhp – some 195bhp/tonne – and together with some weight reduction cut the 0-60mph dash by nearly a second. Inside the car was also closer to the Elise, with all luxuries stripped-out to be replaced with electrical cut-out, roll bar, plumbed-in fire extinguisher and competition seats.

6 Improving
on perfection

The Elise S2 was more evolution than revolution, retaining the familiar look and dimensions of the original car. (Tony Baker)

Take off the rose-tinted spectacles for a moment, step back and take a second look at the Elise in the dim light of a rainy day. It's still great, but you'd be naïve to say that it couldn't be improved. At the October 2000 Birmingham Motor Show, Lotus followed its own precedent and launched an evolution of the Elise, the Series 2, to use past Lotus terminology. The firm has always refined and improved its best models, Elan, Europa and Esprit to name a few, ironing out flaws to further enhance their appeal, and Elise was no exception. 'A car has a life cycle,'

explained Tony Shute. 'It starts off being in great demand and everybody wants it, then after two or three years, particularly when you're in a tight niche like this, a lot of those people have already got their car. What the S2 does is open the field out a bit more.' But the new incarnation stayed true to the original concept, merely building on the qualities of the first car to keep it ahead of the rivals nipping at its heels, including the Lotus-based Vauxhall VX220/Opel Speedster.

The first discussions on the idea of a second generation Elise began in the autumn of 1998, with principle designer Steven Crijns preparing the first sketch for October to boost the business case for the new model. Codenamed Project Monza, yet still listed as Type 111, the S2 was given the green light in March the following year. Although there was to be a huge amount of design work done over the following nine months, the final car stayed remarkably true to the first Crijns sketch.

The S2 has been harshly criticised as simply a reskin, but Crijns was given an extremely tough brief to retain the Elise look, but add purpose, quality and a style to appeal to a larger audience. 'Initially we wanted to do a completely new design, something fresh, something futuristic,' said Crijns, 'because the original Elise sometimes gets criticised for being too retro. Then GM came along and did the VX220, which was very futuristic, we looked at it and thought it wasn't what Lotus should be doing at all. We should stick with what we've got; it's right, it's good and if some people don't like it then tough.' The design team vetoed calls to use the extended

wheelbase of the GM car to allow the two to share chassis, preferring to keep the compact dimensions of the original Elise. But Crijns was keen to get away from the over-friendly looks of the S1 and give a style that told onlookers more about the car's potential. 'The S1 didn't say what kind of driving experience it gave,' said Crijns. 'We did an evolution of the style and gave it a bit more presence on the road, it's a lot more aggressive without being brutal, without being arrogant. The tail was the biggest change, mainly the spoiler but we also wanted to make it a bit more organised with

Steven Crijns experimented with a tail design that was a continuation of the first car's stick-on spoiler. . . (Lotus)

. . . but opted instead to go for an all-new design that integrated the spoiler, broadcast the Lotus name and accentuated the rear diffuser. (Lotus)

The second Elise remained remarkably true in final form to the first sketch of principle designer Crijns. (Lotus)

the number plate, and the Lotus name is a nice name to show off.' A sweeping rear panel gave the room for a chromed 'LOTUS' badge and Crijns designed the new 'Elise' script, as Thomson had for the first car. A curious mix of retro and futuristic, the new Elise managed to retain a familiar Lotus look, but with a taught shape and sharper line more akin to a 'New Edge' design. Intricate, bespoke headlight units showed evolution from the 340R and the M250 styling concept (see Chapter 9), with the indicators as close together as is legally permitted. There were racy details such as a flush-fitting fuel filler cap, and the air intakes on the nose and side were enlarged and accentuated with injection-moulded strakes to make them more of a feature.

Work moved on to the computer in December 1999 once the sketch design had

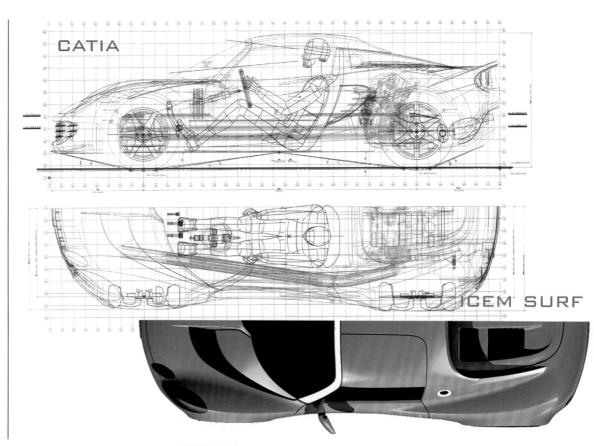

Working with computer-aided design alongside paper and models allowed the project to progress much more quickly than previous Lotus designs. (Lotus)

From the front, Crijns's one third-scale model shows the now-familiar aggressive, sharp-edged Elise S2 look. (Author)

been signed off, which helped the project to be completed in such a short time, although the traditional hands-on approach continued in the production of third-scale models. The chosen model was scanned and the dimensions put into the Catia CAD system, which was then used to mill a pair of full-size clays at the new Lotus Engineering facility in Coventry. One was destined for the studio and the second, complete with functioning air intakes and exits, for wind tunnel testing. After the problems with the Elise S1 aerodynamics, the Lotus Design team was not about to make the same mistakes again. 'First thing we did was go straight to the wind tunnel with the model,' Crijns recalled. 'With a load of clay we determined where the spoiler needed to go and it was shocking to see it right up in the sky, to make it look good was quite a challenge. The reason why it has such a big spoiler is not just about creating downforce, but creating a balance of

The rear view of the completed full-size S2 clay in the studio, with an example of the original Elise. (Lotus)

Principal designer Steven Crijns with the completed Elise S2 full-size clay in the courtyard of the then-new Lotus Design studios. (Author)

downforce between front and back as there is so much at the front with the air dam and bonnet exit.'

In addition to neatly integrating the spoiler into the rear design, the roof and roll bar were lowered and the support bars of the soft-top were altered to improve airflow and reduce drag. The tail was squared off for improved stability and the aluminium rear diffuser accentuated, although the designers were not permitted their preferred carbon-fibre item for cost reasons. 'On the first Elise you can't see the diffuser very well, it's hidden underneath,' said Crijns. 'I think it's a great thing to show off, it's a racy element, so we made it stick out a lot more and moved it a lot higher up to get more efficiency from it.' And the changes were certainly worthwhile. Although the drag coefficient of the S2 was little changed from the S1, 0.407 as opposed to 0.408, in the critical front-to-rear downforce ratio it was streets ahead. The

Crijns's design accentuated the rear diffuser, both for styling and aerodynamic reasons, and the twin exhausts were moved apart. (Tony Baker)

nose of both the S1 and S2 boasted negative lift (downforce) figures of -0.03, but for the S1 the rear lift was positive, at 0.05, while for the S2 it was a much more secure -0.02.

A few of the designers' wishes were scuppered by the law, such as Crijns's desire to have the wheels either flush with the wheelarches or standing proud. Larger diameter rims, 16in fronts and 17in rears, helped fill the arches and a 10mm drop in ride height reduced the gap from wheel top to arch, but to fully comply they had to sit within the bodywork. Crijns was also irked by the problem of adding number plates to the front of his neatly resolved nose. To avoid the plate looking like an afterthought as it had on the S1, he integrated the number plate plinth into the styling, saving weight at the same time. Throughout the design process, the directors of Lotus paid monthly visits to the studio to monitor progress. The clay was covered with Dinoc highlighting film with black tape for the shut-lines and

mock light units to give an idea of final form, and placed alongside an original Elise. There was little argument when it came to sign-off time for the exterior design at Christmas 1999, and with the approval of the board the prototype tooling could begin.

Internal alterations

As with S1, the interior and exterior design programmes ran together, although sign-off for the full-size interior clay was not until Easter 2000. Despite a little more sophistication, the interior of the new Elise retained the classic feel. 'We liked the concept and minimalist look with lots of aluminium on show,' explained Crijns, 'we didn't want to start covering it all up.' But with the number of people using Elises as daily drivers the team had to consider practicality more than they had for the toy-like S1. 'There were quite a few things we wanted to improve, the storage was one so that's why the aluminium shelf on the dashboard happened. We didn't want to make special storage bins, but make use of the structure.' Proposals such as a fussy flip-down cover for the stereo and heater controls were dropped for cost reasons, as was a VX220-style wheel incorporating an airbag.

Probably the greatest internal change was the improved access, thanks to a 50mm bite out of the narrower sill with triangulated sections for strengthening, as found in the GM car, and 40mm longer doors. Crijns came up with a neat way of hiding this blemish in the handsome chassis: 'We didn't like having to cover up this afterthought so we integrated the dashboard design with the cover. That worked well because it made the dash seem really narrow and makes you feel like you're sitting in a single-seater sports car. If you look at the chassis it has a V-shape around you, but in the original Elise you don't really feel that.' The linking pieces between dashboard and sills incorporated front speakers, and there were further changes to the switchgear. Parts-bin components were replaced with hi-tech momentary switches with LEDs to show

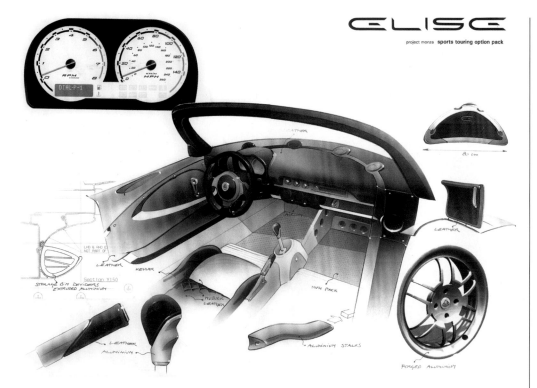

The Sports Tourer specification offered carpets, an adjustable passenger footrest and Nubuck leather trim. (Lotus)

The sportier Race Tech option package featured advanced trim materials and an industrial finish to the footwells. (Lotus)

The Stack instruments were housed in a new binnacle and a redline was added to the rev counter, but the graphics were harder to read.
(Tony Baker)

when they were activated. 'The switchgear on the first car was quite nice, but didn't feel very sophisticated or tactile,' said Crijns. 'There are so many nice products out there like mobile phones or stereos that have good switches.' The Stack instruments were redesigned with a neat new binnacle and less readable new graphics, and Crijns redesigned the door panels so they would no longer accommodate the nasty plastic S1 window winders, forcing a switch to preferred – but rather more costly – aluminium items.

Continuing the theme of practicality, the wider tail allowed for a larger boot, now containing the battery, with improved access, and there was a new hood by Lotus Design. 'It's not as easy to use as an electric hood, but a Mazda MX-5-style hood would be totally inappropriate for this car: too heavy, too over-engineered, it takes too much space and it wouldn't fit,' said Crijns. 'On the first

car it was done quite late into the project because it was supposed to be just a shower cape, it wasn't ever supposed to be a proper roof because we didn't think people were going to use it every day.'

Changes were certainly not restricted to the body, as a five-minute drive in an S2 will confirm. Young and enthusiastic vehicle dynamics engineers Gavan Kershaw and Matt Becker were given the task of improving on the already superb Elise driving experience. 'We had this car that nobody complained about and we had to develop a car to be better, so reputations were really at stake,' recalled Becker. 'We couldn't think of anything else on the marketplace that gave the same kind of response and driver involvement, so the benchmark car was Elise 1.'

The S2 was the first car to be developed on the new and improved Hethel track, and the

108

Wipac headlights mirrored the 340R, with the indicators as close together as legally permitted. (Tony Baker)

Air intakes were enlarged and accentuated with pronounced plastic strakes to make them more of a styling feature and part of the racing car feel. (Tony Baker)

first to really exploit the software capability at Lotus Engineering to reduce development time. The team was able to make use of the RAVEN programme for chassis dynamics, the MICES engine package and the CARPS vehicle system performance simulation, developed in 1999, which could accurately predict performance, economy and emissions before build. But the biggest improvement for Kershaw and Becker was the willingness of associated industries to assist in the new car's development. 'The previous Elise was

The new Lotus-designed six-spoke alloy wheels were larger than those found on the S1, but weighed no more.
(Tony Baker)

initially going to be built in small numbers so getting suppliers on board was difficult because they weren't going to get any money out of it and no-one had heard of it,' said Kershaw. 'But this time around we could guarantee 3,000 cars per year and the Elise was already heralded as one of the best handling cars, so we had Bridgestone, Bilstein and different bush manufacturers saying they wanted to work with us.'

Other than the cut-down sills to aid entry and exit, the actual structure of the chassis was left largely untouched, but unfortunately the clever extruded aluminium suspension uprights were replaced by drop-forged steel items for improved stiffness and durability. To combat the greater unsprung weight, Lotus Design worked with alloy wheel specialist Rimstock on a new, lighter road wheel with a six-spoke design that no longer exposed quite so much of the cast-iron discs. The rims were shod with new Bridgestone Potenza RE040 tyres, developed in association with Lotus. 'The key to development of Elise 2 was the tyres,' said Becker. 'Once Bridgestone were on board to develop both a front and a rear tyre with the characteristics we wanted we could develop the suspension around that. With Elise 1 we had a dominant front tyre and were always trying to get rid of the grip so you compromise spring rates or damper settings.'

Thanks to the light weight of the Elise, Bridgestone was able to develop a much softer compound of tyre in parallel with testing by the guys at Lotus: 'They were on board from the very first time we drove the new Elise,' said Kershaw. 'They'd give us tyres and then go away for six weeks while we'd do damper tuning, springs and roll bars. We'd then meet up again in Rome, put the new tyres on with our new settings and take a step forward.' With the S2, Kershaw and Becker followed the lead of the GM car by specifying wider rear tyres and narrower fronts, albeit with different diameter rims: 'We wanted a 175 front tyre and everyone thought we were mad,' Kershaw explained. 'We were going 10mm narrower at the front, but we knew that the balance would be

Wider track, wider rear tyres and thinner fronts virtually eliminated oversteer so the rear of the S2 always feels solidly planted on the road. (Tony Baker)

Cornering speeds were enhanced by the huge amounts of grip generated by the Bridgestone tyres and body roll was reduced by stiffer springing. (Tony Baker)

about the same. You only have to look at 360 Ferraris; they've got a similar tyre ratio to us, so they're brave enough to say: "This is what the masses want".'

'We were pushing for a wet/dry balance because with a light sports car you generally have fantastic dry grip, but they're a little bit nasty in the wet. We wanted to have exceptional dry grip and also exceptional wet grip. Bridgestone came up with a totally new compound to give us this wet grip performance – the tyres actually squeal in the wet around their handling track. It's a lot less sensitive to throttle corrections, braking in a turn, things like that.' With much more rear grip, the new car has eliminated the S1's tendency for lift-off oversteer, with gentle understeer the prevailing tendency. 'You drive some sports cars and you think, 'This is going to hurt me',' said Kershaw, 'with the S2 the more you drive it, the more it unlocks itself. As you live with your car, you learn to understand it, you learn about the physics of the thing and you can start to trick it. You have to trick the car into the real powerslide stuff, the stuff you see journalists doing, you have to trail brake it and things like that.' As Kershaw continued, the new car had to be designed to cope much better with the daily grind: 'Probably 70 per cent of our customers enjoy their normal driving: the drive to work, the B-roads on Saturday morning for a blast. They don't want to be tired and having a white-knuckle drive on a late night journey home.'

Dynamic development

Alongside the tyre development came all-new Bilstein dampers in place of the first car's Konis, with a clever one-way valve design with different gate technology to separate compression and rebound low speed damping forces. The damper could be tuned much more accurately with hundreds of miles of testing to give the ideal combination of ride quality and body control. 'You typically run about three times more rebound force than compression,' explained Becker, 'because rebound is trying to contain the spring. With the Koni you were stuck with

the same amount of compression and rebound so if you wanted to give the car more body control it would affect the low speed damping and it would give you a very hard ride. That's one of the keys to the way the car feels now, it's got a nice ride because we can increase the rebound to give the body control and keep the compression down to keep the ride comfort as well. It is a unique damper, I don't think anybody else makes a monotube damper that allows you to change compression and rebound separately.'

The new dampers and bushes allowed the Eibach springs to be stiffened by 30 per cent at the front and 25 per cent at the rear, bringing them near the levels of the S1 Sport 190 track car and making the car feel more alert. 'Everyone thinks that we've gone softer because we get a fantastic ride out of the car,' said Kershaw, 'but we've done exactly the opposite. It's testimony to the damper and tyre suppliers. We kept pushing the envelope, every time they gave us a better tyre, we'd make the springs stiffer because we wanted less roll. You go up a spring rate and it's like shedding 100 kilos from the car so it just wants to change direction.'

To improve stability, the rear track was increased by 40mm and the front by 20mm, and the 10mm drop in ride height meant a lower centre of gravity. The engineers also changed the kinematics of the suspension, to alter the wheels' behaviour when under load in a corner and maximise the area of tyre in contact with the road. 'We had negative camber in bump [the wheel under load] so because of the lateral force you have a big contact patch with the ground,' Kershaw explained. 'We also had negative camber in droop [inside wheel] so we didn't get much load. With the new car, we kept the same characteristic of negative camber in bump, but we put positive camber in droop, so you get a much bigger contact patch on the ground at all times. Now when you've turned into a corner and you've got a lot of roll angle on, the power is going through two complete tyres. Before, it was going through one outside one so it was more throttle sensitive.'

Changes were not limited to the suspension, although elsewhere it was refinement rather than revolution. New hubs meant a revised brake disc, which used the same 282mm diameter but boasted a more open vein design with smaller sidewalls to improve cooling. The calipers were unchanged from the S1, but there was a new pad material for better bite and feel, although there was not time within the short development programme to resolve a satisfactory anti-lock braking system.

Although the first S2 prototype had run the Lotus-developed GM engine, as found in the back of the VX220/Speedster, the decision was made to stick with the light and freer-revving Rover K-series, albeit with a Lotus K4 engine management system for better throttle response and lower emissions to meet Euro 3 regulations. The wider track

necessitated bespoke driveshafts in place of the MGF items employed on the S1, and there was also a Lotus-developed on-board engine diagnostics system, allowing dealers to download an engine history report and send it to Lotus at each service. Power was up just 2bhp, and torque boosted by 2lb ft (2.7Nm), but the car felt livelier as Becker explained: 'I think a lot of people were disappointed that we hadn't increased the horsepower, but a lot of the journalists thought we had because the response was a lot better.' The increase in wheel diameter necessitated the standardisation of the close-ratio gearbox found in higher-performance variants of the S1 to avoid the car feeling dead off the line. The new 'box gave a sportier feel, and the engineers made a slight redesign in the linkage and its bushing in an effort to reduce free play in the system.

The K-series engine boasted just 2bhp extra with the Lotus K4 engine management system, but felt livelier thanks to a close-ratio gearbox. Boot space was also improved. (Tony Baker)

Elise S2
marches on

Much like the original Elise, the Series 2 was destined to evolve to maintain public interest, boost sales and retain the status of the little Lotus as the best small sports car available. Derivatives of the new car even followed the S1 in their names, with the first available being the rapid Sport 135 of January 2002. Like the original Sport 135, the S2 boasted a tuned K-series engine producing 135bhp – and a useful 129lb ft (175Nm) of torque – thanks to a reflowed cylinder head, aluminium inlet manifold, noisy, bigger bore stainless steel exhausts and a reprogrammed engine management system. For £1,750 more than the price of a standard car you had a 5mph boost in top speed and 0-60mph in 5.4 seconds. Again, like the first version, the Sport 135 was offered as an upgrade kit to be fitted by dealers or by Lotus Motorsport during the car's build. The chassis and suspension remained unchanged and there wasn't even a fancy set of alloys to mark the upgrade, with just discreet decals on the dash, sides and tail to give the game away. Matt Becker was a big fan of the 135: 'It gives the car more torque and makes it feel a little less breathless at high speeds. The Elise 2 suspension set up could cope quite easily with nearly 200 horsepower and it really is a nice engine, free revving and a nice compromise because it's not too expensive.'

Just two months later at the Geneva Motor Show, came the handsome Elise Type 72, in celebration of the multi-World Championship-winning Type 72 Formula 1 car of the 1970s. Mechanically identical to a standard car, the 72 was, as the S1 49 and 79, merely a cosmetic special edition, mimicking the black and gold 'John Player Special' livery introduced on the Type 72 in 1972. Finished in Starlight Black with gold-painted alloy wheels and heritage laurels on each side, the 72

featured black interior trim livened by gold Alcantara inserts on the seats, steering wheel and door panels, with gold heritage laurels embroidered in the centre of each headrest and a heritage identification plate, based on the chassis plates of the Formula 1 car, mounted on the dashboard. The Type 25 was next in the Heritage collection, named after the revolutionary monocoque Grand Prix car that took Jim Clark to the World Championship in the 1960s. The Elise Type 25 featured British Racing Green paint with twin yellow stripes running from nose to tail, even over the standard hardtop, with black alloy wheels and ruby red perforated upholstery.

In addition to the Type 72, Lotus also introduced a pair of track-only versions of the Elise at Geneva, the Sport 190 and Scholarship cars (see Chapter 4). But of more interest to those punters buying cars to use every day, all year round, were the new optional hardtop and combined heater and air conditioning system. Although hardcore enthusiasts accused Lotus of going soft and betraying the original concept of light weight and minimalism by offering air-con in an Elise, the move was an attempt to appeal to a wider audience, and was a step on the road to federalisation (see Chapter 9). Besides, at just 15kg (33lb) the Lotus-designed £1,295 unit was super-light, although the installation in the centre of the dash was not particularly attractive. The hardtop was another matter, a handsome panel that, with a fluted effect down the centreline, had almost a Zagato-style 'double bubble' effect. Lotus designers had originally pursued a gullwing idea that revived a concept from the Project M111 sketches, but resolving the complicated design proved too time-consuming and it was put on hold. Priced at £1,295, the new lid was shorter, leaving a moulding covering the rear roll bar and merging in with the flying buttresses, and weighed 9.5kg (21lb). A new and much easier and quicker-fitting soft-top accompanied it, also stopping short of the roll bar.

For June 2002 came the S2 incarnation of the hugely popular 111 model, once again using Rover's variable valve control system, but this time developed further by Lotus in-house with a higher compression ratio, a larger intake, a larger throttle body and a clever new resonator, designed to remove harshness and tune the induction noise. There was the Lotus K4 engine management system and the 111 boasted a new exhaust, complete with an internal valve that opened as engine speed passed 4,000rpm to give more noise and power. Peak power of 156bhp came in at a heady 7,000rpm and although 15kg (33lb) heavier at 765kg (1,687lb), the 111 boasted an impressive power-to-weight ratio of 204bhp/tonne which gave outstanding performance when mated to the new G6 gearbox, whose ratios offered more performance off the line as well as longer-legged cruising. Of more interest was the torque, the same 129lb ft (175Nm) as the earlier Sport 135, but delivered some 550rpm lower at 4,650rpm. One surprising bonus of the engine and gearbox modifications was improved economy and lower emissions, the latter putting the 111 in a very low company car tax bracket, providing further appeal.

The chassis and suspension remained unchanged and the alloys, although a smarter and lighter new nickel-polished eight-spoke design, were the same size and shod with the same rubber. Externally, the 111 continued the Elise tradition of subtlety, although there were the dramatic spidery alloys, badges on the sides, tail and rear window and a stylish three-part rear diffuser. The new model was available as the 111, a pure power upgrade with spartan interior and a price tag of £25,995, or for an extra £2,000, there was the plusher 111S with extra spec including leather upholstery and carpets. With an exceptional mix of punch throughout the rev range, economy and refinement, the 111 was without doubt among the most appealing Elise options of all.

As with the S1, the Sport 135 was the first high-performance derivative of the Elise S2. (Lotus)

An Elise Type 72 stands alongside the original Lotus Type 72 Formula One car. The Type 72 was the first of a number of heritage colour schemes planned for the S2. (Lotus)

One of the best all-round Elises, the Elise 111 boasted 156bhp and was also available as the more luxurious 111S. (Lotus)

For Geneva Motor Show 2002 came a compact and lightweight air-conditioning system for the Elise. (Lotus)

By the time the new Elise was ready for the first press reviews, both Kershaw and Becker were confident that they had created a significantly better car. 'We'd had four years of driving Elises and the project team knew the little bits they wanted to change,' concluded Kershaw. 'Hindsight is a wonderful thing, but this time we were actually able to change things for the better, the only thing we kept in the suspension was the steering rack because everyone loved the steering. The new car has got 90 per cent new suspension components, it's got 100 per cent new body panels. We wanted to keep the sizing and the nature of the car, everything else could change, and by changing that many components we could tune what we wanted into it.' Becker was equally proud of what the team had achieved: 'The engineers who were responsible for the ride and handling of Elise 1, people like John Miles and Dave Minter, did the best job that they could with the components they had at the time. We have done the best job that we can with the components we have. Ultimately we wanted the car to be fun. Elise 1 did oversteer a bit too much and it was difficult to get the handling characteristics we wanted out of that car because the dampers were quite restrictive in certain areas. To get the car to feel the way it does is a combination of the tyres, the spring rates, the damping, suspension kinematics, suspension geometry, and also the car was tuned by people that enjoy driving.'

Elise S2 meets its market

The new Elise was developed in impressive secrecy to avoid damaging sales of the S1 car in the run-up to production, so its unveiling in Birmingham was a shock to both press and public. Not that there was anything secretive about the launch, which was in total contrast to the introduction of the S1, with all of the glitz and glamour expected of a new sports car. Flashing lights and scantily clad blondes heralded the arrival of the new Elise, which not even the show programme had been aware of.

Lotus boasted that the new car used 50 per cent new parts and spoke of a gullwing hardtop to follow, with removable panels to leave a targa-style roof. The S2 was destined to go on sale in the UK in late November, but it was April 2001 before customer car delivery began in earnest. Priced just a few hundred pounds above the S1 car at £22,995, the new model broke from tradition by being offered in three definite trim levels, beginning with Standard trim featuring cloth seats and rubber floor mats. For an extra £2,995 there was the sporty 'Race Tech' option pack, complete with industrial-style non-slip metal floor surface, cross-drilled discs, driving lamps, a two-speaker sound system and Alcantara trim, with special Keprotec Kevlar motorbike jacket material on the seat edges for a hard-wearing yet racy look. Top of the range was the 'Sports Tourer' which, at £3,195 more than standard, offered Nubuck leather seats, fascia and door covering, floor carpets, a four-speaker sound system and an adjustable passenger footrest. The options offered in the packs could be bought separately of course, along with black alloy wheels, emergency tyre compound and inflator (different-size front and rear wheels made a spare useless) and bespoke luggage bags. A further difference between the S1 and S2 was that the press reaction to the first car was so good that it never really needed much advertising, becoming a living legend within weeks of its launch. But sales of the new car were boosted by a blaze of publicity, with stylish adverts featuring a ruby red Elise on a black background under the slogans 'not much up top, but a great ride' and 'you only live once, so live life in the fast lane'.

Reactions to the new looks were mixed, some loving the added aggression and road presence, but others, the designer of the S1, Julian Thomson, included, found the detailing a little fussy. 'I do quite like it, but I was disappointed that they changed it so quickly,' commented Thomson, 'it seemed unnecessary. People never make the comparison between the two, but the thing that annoyed me was that we did the whole

Inside, there was marginally less roof-up headroom, but more comfort, refinement and a huge step forward in quality. The car depicted has the Race Tech option pack. (Tony Baker)

original car for about £5 million and they did a new body for £40 million or something like that.' But step aboard a new Elise and it's like moving a light-year on in quality terms. Fit, finish and detailing are much improved, visible in the engine bay where the mess of mastic that held the cooling grilles in place on S1 cars was replaced by neatly installed injection-formed ventilation slats. Inside, only the steering wheel and pedals remained from the original car, with the new moulded sill covers proving easier to clean, less cold as an elbow rest and creating a more intimate feel to the cabin. There were fewer sharp edges and a less plasticky, less kit-car feel to the new switchgear, which included far more stylish and easier to operate alloy heater knobs and delicate back-lit light buttons.

Not that all was perfect. Fitting carpets in an Elise was heresy to the die-hard enthusiasts, so the standard car or the Race Tech option with its funky floor and comfy Alcantara trim were the preferred options for purists. The new graphics for the Stack

instruments were difficult to read due to a stylised script, although at least there was now a redline for the rev counter for the first time. New-style seats were supremely comfortable despite the shallow padding, with a beautifully ergonomic design, although for very tall drivers the car could be cramped, the lower roofline dictating a theoretical limit of 6ft 4in.

On the road, a new fixed rear window and tuned exhaust note made the S2 more refined, more grown-up, but it lost none of the unique Elise driver appeal. If anything, it felt even more responsive, changed direction even more alertly with the same fabulous steering, delightfully weighted and perfectly placed pedals offering a familiar click of metal on metal at their full travel, and even sharper brakes. The already impressive ride quality had improved, with the new car offering astounding stability and greater resistance to road imperfections on a twisty lane. There was less kickback from ruts in the road, but still superb feel through the seat and feedback from the wheel. Thinner front tyres inevitably signalled understeer at the limit, but the staggering levels of grip those special Bridgestones generated meant that at all but life-threatening speeds the handling remained beautifully neutral. The biggest advance in grip came from the rear, which was now virtually unshakeable. If the nose started to push wide, you could back gently off the throttle without fear and it would simply tighten its line. Some of the entertainment value of the first car, which could be easily prompted into a powerslide out of low-speed corners, was now gone, but try hard enough and the new car could be tweaked sideways, although probably an activity best attempted only in the dry. Overall, the new car was both easier to drive and easier to drive fast, offering masses more confidence in the wet.

The few complaints were merely problems with the first car that could not be ironed out with the time and resources available. The exhaust note was still a disappointment and the gearchange, although slightly improved, had a familiarly mushy feel. The close-ratio

transmission made the car feel quicker off the line and always more accelerative, removing any flat spots and adding an urgency at any revs in any gear. But the payback arrived in long-distance motorway driving when the higher-geared top ran the engine at around 1,000rpm higher at the legal limit, which had a knock-on effect on economy.

Building the S2 was a much more sophisticated process, and even nearer to pure assembly than construction. Luke Bennet was in charge of putting Project Monza into production in a brand-new, £7 million three-hall factory built towards the end of 1999 to house both the Vauxhall VX220/Opel Speedster and Elise S2 lines. The new facility had the capability to boost annual production at the newly titled Lotus Manufacturing from a maximum of 3,500 up to a potential 10,000 units per year. Production got under way as the year 2000 drew to a close, with a new manufacturing process for improved quality control as part of the stringent requirements demanded by General Motors for the VX220/Speedster.

With the emphasis on ease and speed of construction to meet the predicted volumes, it soon became obvious that the laborious hand-lay process, which was fine when the car was predicted to be a maximum production of 900 cars per year, would have to be abandoned. In fact, the volume of cars required was considered too much even for the favoured VARI process, so Lotus looked to French firm Sotira to provide panels using its RTM (resin transfer moulding) system. RTM involves loading pre-impregnated matting into polished, chrome-faced steel tools and squeezing male and female moulds together under high pressure. This ensures even panels with much greater strength and quality than hand-lay, allowing them to be thinner. The average thickness of S2 panels was down from 3mm to 2mm, which saved weight, offsetting some gains elsewhere in the car. A disadvantage was that hand-lay allows one large single panel for front or rear, but RTM is fussier with lots of small panels, requiring the designers to allow for shut-lines. Steven Crijns explained: 'It was

The lighter, higher-quality body panels from Sotira in France met the chassis on the all-new production line. (Author)

quite frustrating that the first Elise was such an amazing car but let down by quality, with hand-lay if you opened the doors you could see the fibreglass in the front fender. We were quite keen to do something about those things on the second car and I think we've achieved most of it; there are very few untidy areas. In the hand-lay clamshell you can make lots of undercuts, but when you don't do hand lay it has to be quite simple, that's where all the shut-lines appear on the car, the first car had none. We actually prefer them because it looks more refined, when you don't have any it looks a bit like a toy.'

The panels were shipped to Hethel where they were painted using a special water-based colour developed in conjunction with Du Pont, before they went on to meet the chassis, which was now provided by Hydro's new Worcester plant rather than shipped

from Denmark. Assembly at the new facility was much more like the regimented line you expect to see in a car factory, as the Elises moved from bare chassis to completed car in a logical and visible step process. New assembly tooling included a bonding jig to ensure an accurate body fit, created from the same CAD data employed to make the body moulds. The funky new lights were sourced from Wipac and the vacuum-formed interior trim panels were also bought-in from outside suppliers.

Once all ancillaries had been fitted, each car underwent a full quality audit, with the paint checked in daylight booths, the engine tested on the rolling road, a visit to the spray room to check for water ingress, and the all-important run around the Hethel track. Unfortunately, the stringent quality requirements were so tough that early production was delayed, in particular by the

'No fault forward' system, which stopped the line each time a fault was detected and prevented the car moving forward until the fault was rectified. With as little as two Elises a day rolling off the line, cars were slow to reach dealers and there was soon a six-month backlog on deliveries, with some outlets going bust under the strain. By March 2001, production had begun to pick up, but it couldn't stop 300 redundancies in swathing cutbacks at Hethel.

But once the cars were out on the road, they were soon making some very influential friends. *Auto Express* voted the new Elise its 'Roadster of the Year' for 2001 and, like the S1 had in 1996, the S2 also scooped *Autocar*'s 'Britain's Best Driver's Car' award for 2001. It also matched its predecessor's five-star road test score, with the testers concluding: 'Lotus has done what we thought impossible. It's improved what we

still consider to be the best affordable roadster of all time.' Australian magazine *Motor* was a little more pragmatic: 'Two things the Lotus man told me were that the new car was easier to get in and out of and that the roof was a much better design. I hope his nose stops growing soon.' But evidently it was still won over by the car's charms: 'Lotus seems to have done a pretty convincing job of turning an *enfant terrible* into something just as engaging but without the rough edges.' Despite it lagging in sixth place behind the supercars in *Evo*'s 'Car of the Year' competition, the magazine gave perhaps the best assessment of the car's qualities. 'Like some blinding flash of insight, the Elise cuts right through all the bullshit and pretension and muddy thinking that affects so many cars and goes right to the core of driving . . . Tiny car; big experience.'

Quality control was taken up a level for the new car. Here, an Elise undergoes checks in the daylight booth before a final shakedown on the track. (Author)

7 Living with the Elise

All sorts of people have invested in an Elise, from 20-something track day enthusiasts to McLaren technical director Adrian Newey, who created a dramatic carbon-fibre bodied and turbocharged machine with some 300bhp. There were also the 40-plus family men with a bit of disposable income looking to rediscover the joys of a proper sports car at weekends without having to resort to the unreliability of a classic.

Although it was already excellent value in performance-per-pound terms, the Elise still remained tantalisingly out of reach for many. Some owners went abroad in an effort to save cash on the list price, but reluctance

from European dealers and the hassle factor of arranging the sale – not to mention the possible delays – made it barely worthwhile. Another way to make an Elise a more viable option, particularly popular among younger buyers, was to buy on finance, and in 1999 Lotus introduced Lotus Finance Ltd, a collaboration between Group Lotus and Chartered Trust plc, offering packages to help finance a new Lotus. There was Asset Purchase, with a fixed rate of interest and repayment over a specified period. Or there was the Preferences package, offering the opportunity to swap for a new Lotus every two or three years, pay the full amount and

Whichever incarnation of the Elise you opt for, be prepared for lots of fun at a very reasonable price. (Tony Baker)

keep the car, or return it and pay the difference between the amount owing and a previously agreed Guaranteed Future Value.

A limited number of Series 1 Elises were bought as company cars, but with the S2, and particularly the plusher Sports Tourer which offered a realistically comfortable daily driver, there came a big push in this lucrative sector. With change in company car taxation to benefit cars with low emissions in the UK's 2002 budget, the ball was firmly in the Lotus court. With the impressively low 177g/km CO_2 of the standard car, and even lower figures for the more powerful 111, tax was almost halved for 2002/3 to just 17 per cent, making it cheaper than some very bland Euroboxes, not to mention being well under half the amount commanded by a Porsche Boxster.

The fear for many as the Elise hit the market was the combination of an all-new construction method and the Lotus reputation for fragility and unreliability – not for nothing was the acronym 'Lots Of Trouble, Usually Serious' coined. When the Esprit was launched, for example, new owners suffered from fuel leaking on to the

coil and causing fires, seizing of the rose-jointed suspension, and the pop-up headlamps retracting unexpectedly at night. But although the Elise suffered the odd gremlin, in Lotus terms it was actually impressively reliable. Major failures included problems with cars jamming in gear, throttles sticking on, thanks to problems with the throttle regulator and throttle body, or broken rear springs after just 12,000 miles which required the whole car to be fitted with modified items. More annoying than debilitating were grievances such as window winders that stiffened then refused to work at all, S1 boot release catches that offered little security and didn't function as they should, hood complaints including worn canvas, broken fitting clips and roll bar covers which came apart at the seams. Julian Thomson bought himself a metallic black year 2000 example of the car he designed, but used it little and sold it in early 2002. 'I only did about 1,000 miles in it,' he explained, 'I've got two kids and when I got to go and play with cars the Dino usually took preference. And every time I went out for a drive [in the Elise] it had a flat battery, which I found

Lotus hoped the Elise would finally rid it of the acronym 'Lots Of Trouble, Usually Serious'. (Tony Baker)

From **Caterham** to Elise: a **sprinter's** tale

Motoring journalist Steve Cropley was one of a number of Caterham owners to be attracted to the Elise by its combination of usability and driver appeal. 'It was because of the sprints and hill-climbs I do with my kid Jon,' Cropley explained. 'He's very tall and has large feet and neither of us could drive the Caterham in anger with our shoes on, not even with driving boots. When you're trying to get the best out of the car and the difference between a bad time and a good one is half a second, not being able to use the pedals properly is a pain. So we tried the Elise and it was much roomier for the pair of us. I wanted something a bit more civilised and modern that would ride well, and I was around for the entirety of the Elise's gestation so I felt involved with the car.'

Cropley swapped his 1990 Caterham 1700 Super Sprint, complete with 160bhp Ford crossflow engine, for a 1997 Elise 1.8i. Bought in late 2000 for the princely sum of £12,500, the 36,000-mile Monaco-registered car was pressed into service in up to ten sprints and hill-climbs a year at venues such as Shelsley Walsh, Wiscombe Park, Prescott, MIRA and Curborough. But use was not restricted to competition as Cropley said: 'It's much

better to live with, my wife can drive it to work and I get it out on Sundays and go for a blast. It lives in a dry garage and it only gets driven on nice days so it has the ideal life, I don't do more than 3-4,000 miles a year.'

To boost grip and reduce roll, Cropley added 111S wheels with Yokohama tyres and a Dynamic Suspensions handling kit: 'It's closely related to the Exige suspension except everything's a bit calmer, so there's not too much banging and crashing,' he said. 'But it's highly adjustable, you can have it hard as hell or really quite compliant, I mainly adjust it for wet and dry and it seems to work. In raw terms the spring rates are 40 per cent stiffer, but the ride is still very flat and compliant. If I had an Elise just for road use I would make these mods anyway, but it's expensive at £500 a corner.' Despite disappointing power-to-weight after the Seven, Cropley was reluctant to uprate the standard K-series: 'I'm really torn because the engine has done 45,000 miles and it's really sweet. It gets good economy and it feels fast on the road; it feels torquey too, you can pull away from 2,000rpm and at Wiscombe Park it was as easy to pull out of the hairpins in second as it was in first, and they are really slow, 20mph [32km/h] at most. They say the 135 is good because it retains the relaxed nature of the engine, but I'm kind of keen on the idea of the Turbo Technics blower. The 160s don't seem to add a great deal and even 190s seem to be not very torquey and not very durable, I've certainly seen some smoky Exiges on sprints. People always say that you can go much quicker by getting your technique right, so I've come to the conclusion that I'll just leave it. But it's a

bit galling to have a 118bhp engine when various blokes in the competition say their cars are standard Elises, but what they mean is a Sport 135 or a 160, and they wonder why I'm a second and a half slower.'

Unlike many S1 owners, Cropley was not tempted to upgrade to the newer S2. 'I'm particularly keen on the Mk1 'classic' body,' he said, 'I think it's much prettier, more in keeping with Lotus heritage.' He is not blind to the car's faults though, as he explained: 'The one thing that has annoyed me the most is the propensity for stonechips. It was chipped around the nose and down the sides when I bought it and it's worse now. Some of the screwheads are rusty and those little mesh grilles at the back are pretty grotty, but I've got no problem with the quality at all, as long as you keep the nuts tight. Plus, it seems to do 30-something to the gallon and with me being older the insurance is pretty cheap.'

As a long-time Lotus fan and former owner of an Elan +2S 130, Elan Sprint and Excel, Cropley has found the Elise an entirely different experience: 'It's modern, it's reliable and it starts every time.' He feels it compares well with Lotus's heritage: 'One of the major motivators for me in owning the car was that I admired everything that Colin Chapman did. The older I get, the heavier cars get because everything you test drive now is full of crash structure and always weighs 100kg more than the last one. Then along comes this car in the mid-'90s which is amazingly light and furthermore, through at least one iteration manages to keep its light weight. I think Colin Chapman would have admired that a great deal.'

really irritating, I just lost faith in it.'

Probably the best advertisement for Elise reliability was the car loaned to *Autocar* magazine for long-term test. Used as a track day tool, a daily driver and a Continental tourer, the car visited Scotland, Germany, France and Switzerland on its way to covering over 50,000 miles in less than two years. In that time it cost just £1,784 in servicing – incredibly reasonable for a

performance car from one of the most exotic names in motoring. More impressive was the fact that, no matter how much the squeaks and rattles annoyed, the car never let them down, despite becoming one of the highest mileage cars on the fleet. Like most, the *Autocar* Elise didn't escape modification, with a hardtop, sports exhaust and 135bhp engine upgrade, but an 'off' at the Nürburgring cost the magazine dear, a front

Motoring journalist Steve Cropley was one of a number of Caterham Seven owners to be tempted into the Elise for sprint and hill-climb thrills. (Tom Wood)

end rebuild back at the factory stung at £6,500. The road testers also discovered quite how sensitive an Elise is to the tiniest change to its set-up. As the rear tyres wore – each set lasting little more than 10,000 miles – the handling was substantially altered. But when lift-off oversteer became scary the car was returned to the factory, where it was discovered that the front axle bump steer and the tracking were well out, hence the problem. More worrying was the dramatic imbalance caused by a loose ball joint in the rear suspension, but this fault was the subject of a factory recall, so most cars should avoid the same problem.

As the magazine found, running an Elise over large mileages needn't cost the earth, particularly because, in sports car terms, the Elise is surprisingly gentle on its tyres and brakes. 'The car's brakes are well up to requirements,' said Lotus dealer Bobby Bell. 'Track day use will wear the pads, but pad life is very good. They don't really gobble up anything, they are very light on tyres

considering the performance.' And even if you do need the odd replacement part, there are websites such as www.Eliseparts.com set up to cater specifically for the little Lotus.

Perhaps the most pleasant surprise is how little time you need to spend at the petrol pumps when you run an Elise. 'People are amazed at how little fuel you use when you go to the circuit,' said ride and handling guru Matt Becker. 'When we did the Elise 1 we went on a trip to Chamonix and drove for an hour at 70mph [113km/h] to record fuel economy – we got 59.6mpg [4.7 litres/100km]. The new car is not quite as good as the old one fuel economy wise because of the gearbox. People always say "I bet that costs a lot to run", but the fuel economy is excellent and they're pretty reliable – there's not much to replace. The engine and transmission are extremely reliable and the suspension and the rest are all tough.' But superb fuel economy is nothing new for a Lotus. While the fact that an Elise will easily return 40mpg

Hood removal from the early Elise is a bit of a pain, and with its side bars, supports and flapping canvas is reminiscent of the system found on early Type 26 Elans. (Tony Baker)

For the S2, the hood was redesigned to give a much simpler system and an improved fit. (Tony Baker)

Living with **an Elise** *in Europe*

So what's it like to buy and live with a Lotus Elise if you live outside the UK? Gothenburg architect Heikki Särg ordered a new left-hand-drive 111S from local Swedish Lotus agent, Nya Wendels Bil & Motor Ab. 'It takes a couple of months, but it's not too difficult,' he said. 'I ordered it in January 2000 and got it in June. There are quite a few Elises in Sweden, some people go over to Germany to buy them.'

But why would a Swede be bothered to wait five months for this unorthodox sports car rarity? 'I've always been interested in British sports cars,' Särg explained, 'My first proper car was a Morgan. I'm fond of Lotus and I had an Elan turbo [M100] that was stolen at the end of '98. I also like Lotus Sevens so I thought of a Caterham, but then I looked at the Elise and it was a bit more of a car and a bit more modern. I bought the 111S because it has a little more power.'

Särg covers around 1,500km (900 miles) annually, using the car for fun and for the daily commute around town in the summer. 'I use it every day, but have another car to use during the winter when the weather is bad. If you have a Lotus then you have to understand that when it rains you get wet inside, if you don't want that then buy a Japanese car. But I can stand it, it's worth it because I like the driving experience, it's great fun.' Like most Elise owners, Särg has taken his car on to the circuit for track days and events. 'I have an amateur licence, and have practised with it on a course,' he said, pointing out that he is a member of the Lotus Car Club of Sweden and chairman of his local Sportsvagnsklubben Göteborg (Gothenburg Sports Car Club).

Showing the kind of enthusiasm this car generates, Särg and a group of like-minded Lotus owners made a pilgrimage to the UK in May 2002 to visit Group Lotus headquarters in Hethel, before joining fellow enthusiasts from all over Europe at the Club Lotus 2002 Exhibition at Donington Park. On this trip, as in daily use, the Elise was very reliable, although like many owners Särg has not been able to resist making the odd modification. 'The worst problem is that the idling is not quite right. I have changed the throttle body, but I think it is something else,' he said. 'But the car has not let me down at all and I have bought street slicks [soft-compound tyres] for it and a competition silencer and inlet manifold.'

Särg may not follow the crowd in Sweden, but his enthusiasm for the car may rub off on further European sports car fans, and he confirms that the Elise is a car that he will not part with – thieves beware.

Heikki Särg, a Swede who has a 111S, is one of a growing number of Elise owners in mainland Europe. (James Elliott)

Improving
on the
Elise

When enthusiasts buy your car it boosts the coffers, but when fellow professionals invest, it's more of a compliment. Formula 1 aerodynamicist Steve Pearse was one of those buyers: 'When I was leaving university, I was thinking about doing my own aerodynamic car as an advert to get into F1. The structural side and layout of the car I was drawing was very much like an Elise, although I knew almost nothing about it at the time. I went to look at one some years later when I could afford it, had a test drive in a friend's car and decided it was exactly what I wanted.' Pearse bought his standard '98 Elise in early 2001 with under 20,000 miles on the clock and fell in love with it straight away: 'Drive an ordinary car and it's like sensory deprivation compared to driving an Elise. The thing about an Elise is that it's a sports car through thought, not brute force and ignorance like a lot of sports cars. You've got that lovely precision and wonderful response, I don't want some comfortable wallowy old barge that takes the fun out of driving.' Although it was bought as a second car, Pearse pressed the Elise into daily service and covered some 21,000 miles (33,800km) in just 16 months, fittingly clocking its 40,000th mile (64,360km) during a track day session at the Nürburgring, and eventually decided to sell his theoretical everyday car as it was not being used. 'I tend to drive an extra long route to work in the morning just to

have a bit of fun on the way,' he explained. 'On sunny days I just get the map out in the morning and try to find some wiggly roads, I've become an honorary biker with my friends at work because I use it in the same way.'

Much as he loved the standard car, track days at Goodwood and the 'Ring persuaded Pearse to make his Elise a little bit special. 'You drive the car initially and you think it's fantastic, so much better than any car you've ever driven,' he explained. 'But after about a month and a half you become immune and want slightly more.' That 'slightly more' turned into the cost of the car again in lowered and reworked suspension, motorsport brakes, 160bhp engine upgrade and Speedline light alloy wheels with Advan A038 road/track tyres. 'When you take a passenger in your Elise it always feels incredibly slow,' said Pearse, 'now with a passenger in it's quicker than a standard car when you're by yourself.' Pearse avoided more obvious factory options in tailoring his Elise: 'I got the Bell & Colvill 160 kit because it's such a flat and broad torque curve. It comes on cam at about 4,000rpm, pulls harder and harder to 5,000rpm then stays the same all the way to 7,000rpm. The suspension has been entirely redone with uniball rear toe link, and the bushes have been replaced with much stiffer ones because that's part of where the quirky handling characteristics come from. It has two-way adjustable Dynamics dampers, adjustable front anti-roll bar and some Pilbeam steering arms that get rid of all the bump steer so the steering is absolutely beautiful, it doesn't waver about when you hit the brakes.' But the tyres were the biggest transformation, as Pearse explained: 'You have so much more precision on turn-in

and there's no tread block to bend over before you start to pick up grip. There is a huge amount of grip on the circuit, when they get hot they are just fantastic, and very progressive as well so you can really play about. A038s are lots of fun but very scary in the wet, it can aquaplane as low as 30mph [48km/h] if you're not careful.'

Unusually for an uprated car, Pearse's Elise retained a standard transmission. 'One of the things I'm after is a six-speed 'box,' he said, 'Particularly on track days you get caught between second and third; a closer ratio 'box solves that but then you can't cruise on motorways so a six-speed is the answer.' But the changes transformed Pearse's Elise into a stunning road car and serious track weapon. 'It is hilariously stable at 80-90mph [129-145km/h] through S-bends, drive any other car through at 60mph [96.5km/h] and that's hairy. At Goodwood we were holding Subarus in a straight line and then destroying them through corners.'

But despite all the modifications, Pearse saw his car very much as work in progress and planned to use his professional talents next to improve its aerodynamics. 'I look on it as a car that I can keep developing. Having been to Goodwood you see that the slowest part of the circuit is 60mph so any kind of aero is going to be useful. There will be a front splitter, the diffuser will grow and there will probably be a knife-edge running down the side of the floor.' But true to Chapman's principles, Pearse wants to keep the weight to a minimum by making the new additions in carbon and Kevlar: 'I don't want to put anything on the car that's going to make it heavier without adding performance.'

(7 litres/100km) – and even with *Autocar*'s lead-foot road testers behind the wheel it managed to average over 36mpg (7.9 litres/100km) – is very impressive, it was a figure the Elite could match back in 1957. The Elise also manages to earn itself additional brownie points in its impressive accident resistance and its strong second-hand value. When the S2 was released, S1

prices took a bit of a dive, but they remained strong and CAP predicted residuals of 46 per cent for the new model after three years and 60,000 miles – better than a similarly priced Mercedes C-class.

But buying a car and living with it are undoubtedly two very different things, and there is no doubt that the Elise has sufficient foibles to test the patience of even

Aerodynamicist Steve Pearse has turned his standard Elise into a Porsche-eater, seen here after a trip to the Nürburgring. (Author)

Thanks to the excellent fuel consumption of the Elise, you shouldn't need to use the beautiful aluminium filler cap too often. (Tony Baker)

After early cars suffered from reflections at night, the rear screen of later S1 and all S2 cars was angled to prevent this problem. (Tony Baker)

The new Lotus generation

Kashif Khan is one of a new group of young, affluent Lotus owners attracted to the Hethel marque by the Elise, his first Lotus and first sports car. 'I never had any interest in Lotus before the Elise, but I liked it as soon as I saw it and knew that when I had the cash I was going to buy one,' said the information technology consultant.

Khan looked at the Audi TT and BMW Z3 before buying his ex-demonstrator S2 Elise Sports Tourer at the age of just 23. 'The performance and handling appealed to me,' he said, 'A friend got one and I went out in it and got the feel of what it was all about. I was going to buy an S1, I liked the looks, but it had gone when I got there so I went out in the S2 and was sold

on it. I wasn't as keen on the cat-like S2 styling, but it grew on me and I much prefer it now.' Despite originally wanting an S1, Khan found the S2 to be a better car: 'It's very efficient on fuel, it certainly gets more attention than the S1 and it has a bigger boot. The hood is easier too, it's really straightforward, folds away neatly and it doesn't leak.'

Khan covered some 11,000 miles in his first year of ownership, finding out the pleasures of owning an enthusiasts' car: 'The Lotus wave is quite fun, it makes you feel like you're part of a family.' Unlike most owners, Khan's car remains standard and as yet he has not ventured out on a track day, though he admits to finding the lure of the circuits hard to resist.

As his only car, the Elise offered Khan the trials of running a focused drivers' car day-in, day-out. 'Ventilation is one of the worst things about it – and the handling in bad weather. It's nice around town, but it has a tendency to heat up to around 100-110 degrees very quickly. The day I bought the car I lost the key and the spare

was in the boot. The AA and one locksmith wouldn't touch it, so another came out and had to break in and then make a copy.'

Khan's Elise was unlucky enough to rapidly go through two clamshells, once after hitting a fox and again after a spin in heavy rain on the motorway put it into the central reservation. Unfortunately Khan's enthusiasm for Lotus was tarnished after waiting five months to get his car back after its second clamshell. But he remains a huge fan of the Elise: 'I still drive it pretty much all the time, but now when the weather is bad I give it more respect. I think when they designed the Elise, both S1 and S2, they did a really good job. It's all about power on the take-off – not top speed – and the handling is exceptional. I'm not sure I'd call it a sports car, I'd say it's a racing car. It sits so low, the ride is hard and the interior is very basic.'

And it looks like being a permanent fixture in Khan's driveway: 'As long as I can afford it I'll keep it, but as a second car because it's pure fun.'

130

Elise S2 owner Kashif Khan is one of a new generation of Lotus drivers attracted to the marque by the Elise. (Author)

The Elise has gathered an enthusiastic following both among marque aficionados and newcomers. Club Lotus has even formed a special Team Elise *to cater for the model.*
(Club Lotus)

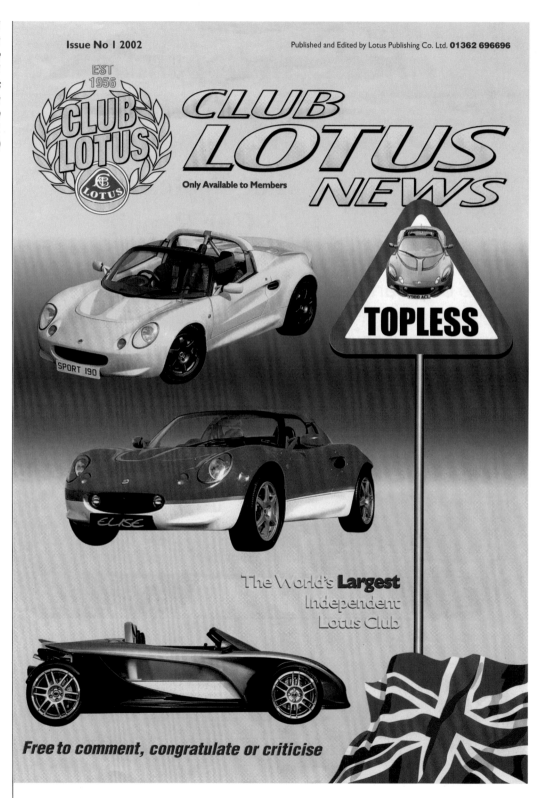

the most dedicated fan. The hood has been a subject of heated debate since the car hit the road in 1996. Series 1 cars undoubtedly suffer from a hood that is patently too difficult to be practical, recalling the lift-the-dot fasteners, poppers and tent-frame constructions of 1960s British sports cars. Most owners have taken to leaving the hood at home and fitting a hardtop for the winter and carrying a 'shower cap' cover in summer to sling over the cockpit when parked. There is no doubt that the new design of hood for the S2 made a huge difference, although it is even easier to break into. One thing is pretty much guaranteed and yet accepted with good grace by most owners: the single-skin canvas hood of the S1 and the S2 will

leak, but usually only a little through the corners of the side windows. Another complaint for those who expect creature comforts is that when it rains, negotiating that sill is guaranteed to get you dirty – pitch up in an Elise to take your date to the ball, and you will not be popular.

One of the difficulties with building such a focused drivers' car is that the passenger does tend to get a bit forgotten. If you are having a blast behind the wheel it's easy to forgive the boominess on the motorway, the occasionally crashing suspension, the hard but wonderfully supportive seats, or the complete inability to hear the radio when pressing on. But for the passenger it's asking a bit much, particularly as they sit in a fixed seat, with no grab handles, and most likely a

The Elise was instantly accepted by Lotus enthusiasts and soon became a regular fixture at club meetings, such as here at the Club Lotus Festival 2002 at Donington Park. (James Elliott)

It was inevitable that owners would indulge in a bit of friendly competition, and here an Elise S1 is prepared for an outing at the 2001 Abingdon Sprint.
(Author)

couple of bags of luggage at their feet. Further complaints of the interior have been levelled at the lack of sun visors, the fabric sill pads and seat edges that wear through, the useless interior lighting, or the pretty but squeaky pedals. Harder to resolve were complaints from buyers of the higher-powered variants who found that without revving the cars to kingdom come there was little improvement in real-world performance on the road.

Clubbing together

One advantage of the huge enthusiast base among Elise owners is that the model has an active club scene. Organisations such as the

Official Lotus Club, Club Lotus and Lotus Drivers' Club offer regular weekend meetings, track days, foreign tours and racing, sprint and hill-climb championships. Instant acceptance of the Elise by enthusiasts helped it fit straight into Lotus culture, and Club Lotus also created 'Team Elise', a separate section dedicated to Elise owners and organising Elise days and technical forums. One bonus of having a VX220 is that the car, although seen as something of a lesser sibling of the Elise, is an entry to both Vauxhall and Lotus worlds, and examples of the GM car are not unheard of appearing at Lotus club meetings.

While the number of owners using their

cars every day has surprised the designers of the Elise, it was inevitable that the large proportion would hammer around circuits on weekend track days.

The timing of the launch of the Lotus showed serendipity as it met a new wave of track day enthusiasts, keen to enjoy the performance of their cars away from congested town roads. 'At any circuit day there are loads of Elises, and a high percentage of them are 135s, Sport 160s and 111Ss,' said ride and handling engineer Matt Becker. 'The nice thing is that you can go there, embarrass a lot of cars that are four times more expensive and leave at the end of the day with your brakes

intact and your tyres hardly scrubbed, so it's an easy and cheap way for people to enjoy circuits.' Lotus road cars have always been taken to the track by privateers, from the days of the original Elite when Les Leston's DAD 10 would be seen regularly dicing with Graham Warner's LOV 1. For the Elise owner, competition is the inevitable next step. So it is no surprise that sprint, hill-climb and amateur sports car racing paddocks since 1996 have frequently boasted healthy showings of the mid-engined Lotus baby, and even more so after the launch of more focused machines such as Sport 190, 340R and Exige.

The Exige simply moved the game forward, offering more power and more grip to cut down those times and an example is depicted on the start line at the 2001 Abingdon Sprint. (Author)

⑧ A shopper's guide

So you know how the Elise came to be, how rewarding it is to drive and what it's like to live with. But how do you buy the right one? There has been a bewildering array of variations and specifications produced and although the aluminium and composite Elise won't rust – steel rear subframe excepted – its unique concept and construction bring with them other problems that a prospective owner needs to be aware of before taking the plunge.

The first point to note is that Elise condition tends to vary dramatically depending on how the car has been driven, and where. Whether it has been abused or not is far more important than the mileage it

There is a bewildering variety of Elise specifications available, not to mention variations such as the Exige. (Tony Baker)

has covered, the used car buyer's favourite guide, as the flyweight Elise is very gentle on its suspension and running gear when driven sensibly, and most standard wear and tear items are both cheap and relatively easy to replace. Because of its stunning performance and handling, the Elise has been snapped-up by many a budding Schumacher to thrash around the circuits, yet on the other hand there are the city types who buy it more as a fashion accessory, covering paltry mileages in stop-start traffic. Either way, an HPI check is always a sound investment to make sure your dream car has not been stolen or written off, and that it does not have a bill of outstanding credit hanging over it.

After six years of production, prices for the cheaper, early cars found a base level of around £13–14,000 for good examples. Bobby Bell, director of Bell & Colvill plc, which has been specialising in Lotus cars since the late 1960s, explained why depreciation was so low: 'The first two years of production were tiny numbers so there are not many early – and therefore cheap – cars around. The competition among buyers to get an entry-level Elise keeps a floor on prices.' Of course, with it being a roadster, Elise values are subject to fluctuations depending on the weather, so a car sold in mid-summer is always likely to make a premium over one sold during the depths of winter.

Values of earlier cars took a dip each time a new, more desirable model was launched, such as the introduction of the 111S in March 1999. But Bobby Bell saw the S2 as the biggest factor in the future of Elise

Buyer's *10-point* checklist

1 Chassis: check carefully for any signs of accident damage or repairs executed by anyone other than a Lotus-approved specialist.

2 Underside: be wary of rippling or damage to the aluminium floor, look for oil leaks and check the rear subframe for corrosion and cracks.

3 Engine: look for a full Lotus service history, check oil and coolant levels and look out for signs of overheating or a blown head gasket.

4 Transmission: check for weak synchromesh, for poor selection due to worn or badly adjusted linkage, and stiff clutch pedal operation.

5 Suspension: rattles, clonks and loose feel indicate tired bushes and shocks, poor tracking and vibration can mean past accident damage which upsets suspension geometry.

6 Brakes: check for scoring of the expensive metal matrix composite discs on early cars; look for excessive wear on cast-iron discs.

7 Body: be wary of cracks or badly mismatched paint, look for the chips, scratches and tears of an unloved car. Ensure that costly headlamp covers and spotlamps are not cracked.

8 Interior: check the sill trim for damage, ensure the hood is intact and window mechanisms work smoothly. Watch for bent keys and bubbling dashboard covers on S2s.

9 VHPD engine: listen out for rattles and look for blue smoke, check the service history for regular attention and check oil condition. If it has covered a high mileage, expect bills.

10 Modifications: make sure that any modifications added to the car are tasteful and executed by recognised specialists or they can affect the value.

second-hand values: 'The Mk2 is going to be much more durable than the Mk1,' he said. 'It is much better built and the problems we have had are with rattles from the extra trim rather than cars not working. The body panels are more uniform thickness thanks to the spray-lay method replacing hand-lay.' But there is also every chance that the purity of the original car's concept will see buyers in the future paying a premium to buy a purist S1 Elise.

As with any market, there will always be a selection of cars advertised below the accepted base. But if something looks too good to be true it usually is, so be wary of apparently very cheap cars. Another factor that can make a dramatic difference to prices is the capacity for personalising the Elise. Few cars remained in standard trim for long after leaving the factory, and prices vary according to taste, quality and desirability of the modifications fitted. Lotus Motorsport-approved options are revered and may add value, while lesser-known and less respected additions can spoil both the looks and purity of the Elise and have a detrimental effect on resale price. They can also act as an indicator of how the car has been used, if a car has been totally hot-rodded, the chances are it will have been driven accordingly.

Of the Elise-based variations, the Exige suffered initially with hefty depreciation due to its fixed roof and no-compromise approach making it a much harder car to live with. But prices soon settled to around £5,000 above Elises of a similar age and condition, and with less than 600 cars built, the Exige is one model that should hold its value due to its rarity and sheer desirability. The 340R was expensive new and has always been seen as a pure toy, an extravagance that represents the most outrageous incarnation of the Elise. This status meant buyers had to pay a premium from the start, and this looks likely to remain the case with survivors of the 340 cars built commanding top prices among the used Elise selection. Although not strictly a Lotus, the blood brother Vauxhall VX220/Opel Speedster deserves a mention simply for the potential of picking up a bargain. Without the Lotus brand identity, *Car* magazine projected residuals at 42 per cent over three years or 36,000 miles in 2001, well below par when compared with an Elise. But considering its qualities, if you can get past the badge on the nose a used VX220 represents huge value and a possible sleeper for the future classic car market.

When looking at any Elise-based model, the most important factor to consider will be the condition of the chassis. The integrity of this incredibly stiff extruded and bonded aluminium structure should be the pass or fail criteria for any prospective purchase. As

Make sure your prospective purchase remains completely flat and unblemished underneath, as ripples in the floor can be a sign of structural damage.
(Author)

the years roll by and early cars remain as rigid and strong as ever, the Elise and its clever chassis are proving the sceptics wrong with the longevity of the concept and others, such as Morgan's BMW V8-powered Aero 8 and the Lotus-developed Aston Martin Vanquish, have followed down the bonded aluminium route. Chassis designer Richard Rackham will defend the concept to the hilt. 'I'm not aware of any problems,' he said. 'We've worked on some other very serious cars using the same technology and the clients in those cases have really put our stuff under scrutiny to make sure they are not going to have a car which comes apart.'

Thanks to the strength of the main tub, and the effectiveness of the composite crash structure, an Elise can suffer apparently huge damage yet remain reparable and retain its integrity. But if an accident – or track day 'off' – is serious enough to damage the chassis, it cannot be welded back together like a conventional car as the bonding of the structure is a carefully controlled process.

Damage to the chassis means the car should be written off or the whole tub replaced, which, with the price of the chassis and the 120 hours labour required to fit it, puts the price of the job up to five figures. However, unscrupulous garages have been known to repair accident-damaged chassis, completely against Lotus instructions. With this in mind, and with the quantity of the chassis that is accessible and visible, the structure should be examined carefully and if anything looks out of place then walk away. Look out for mismatched adhesives, attempts to hide repairs with silver paint, buckling and rippling or evidence of any attempts at welding.

Get the car up on a ramp and inspect its flat aluminium floor and engine cover, complete with NACA ducts to cool the engine. The floor should be absolutely flat, save for a faint cross added to all but the first cars for additional stiffening, so beware of undulations. Inspect the surface for damage too, as debris on the motorway has been known to kick up and rip holes in the

Inspect the subframe for cracks around the rear wishbone and toe-link mounts. (Author)

aluminium. If possible, remove the engine cover to check for serious leaks and to inspect the steel rear subframe. This is the only structural element that can rust so look for the telltale orange corrosion, but also look out for buckling caused by severe impact with potholes or indeed other cars. In particular, check for cracks around the wishbone mounts. This is not a dramatic problem as the subframe itself can be unbolted and replaced, but should be taken into account.

With the Elise, Lotus once again demonstrated the advantages of fitting a mass-produced engine and gearbox, in this case the light, well-proven and eminently tuneable Rover K-series. In general, this is an effective and reliable unit, although early cars in particular suffered from blown head gaskets due to overheating. 'They don't like being cooked,' explained Bobby Bell, 'if they have then the chances are that the head gasket will go.' Overheating is usually a result of lack of coolant, so regular level checks are needed as it has been known to

Look out for corrosion in the rear subframe, the only steel part of the structure. (Author)

Electronic *Elise*

Can't afford an Elise? Then a computer game may possibly be as near as you are going to come to getting behind the wheel, for as little as £20. For the dedicated Lotus enthusiast, the first choice must be *Lotus Challenge*, developed for Virgin Interactive by KUJU Entertainment in conjunction with Lotus itself, for the PlayStation 2 and X-Box games consoles.

Vehicle dynamics engineer Gavan Kershaw helped the programmers make the cars perform realistically. 'Because they digitised the Hethel track it's the ideal benchmark,' he explained. 'You can say: "We'd be doing 95mph [153km/h] through this corner in third gear with a little bit of oversteer." They'd set the gearing and you could change up to 50 parameters. We got the spring rates and tyre sizes for each car and all of a sudden the cars started to drive like the real thing. But we went too far because when they first launched it to the games journalists they couldn't drive it. They wanted something where they could just lob it in and powerslide, so they've put driving aids in. If you turn all the driving aids off the car drives like a road car, but to start with there's traction

control and ABS and all that.' Evaluation engineer Alastair McQueen was also involved: 'We spent a lot of time trying to get it as authentic as possible,' he said. 'We did a lot of filming and recording of vehicle behaviour so they could interpret it, then we looked at it in stages during the development.' The game offers the opportunity to drive anything from an early Lotus Seven through Grand Prix cars to every variation of Elise, including Exige, 340R and S2. In addition to traditional arcade racing, with the unique opportunity of taking to the Hethel test track, the game also features a 'Story Mode', following a fictional Lotus Challenge Team in a world championship and performing stunts for films and advertisements. The handling characteristics are impressively realistic but the game itself, particularly in two-player mode, can feel a bit slow. Go off and the tyres pick up dirt, working themselves clean once back on the track, but the realism takes a break when you have an accident, as sparks fly off the glassfibre and dents appear as if it were steel.

Among the best and certainly the most popular games featuring the Elise are the *Gran Turismo* series from Sony Computer Entertainment for the PlayStation and PlayStation 2. First released back in May 1998, it offers superb graphics, exceptional realism and great fun. As in real life, in the *Gran*

Turismo games, a well-driven Elise will see off far more powerful machinery, either in championship Gran Turismo mode or with one or two-player quick races in arcade mode. *Gran Turismo 2* followed in February 2000, by which time the original had become the best-selling racing game of all time. The new version, by Polyphony Digital, picked up where the old one left off, adding the sights and sounds of the awesome Motorsport Elise and 111S to the range of 13 Lotus models available. The individually tailored handling properties made the Elise a dominant force and the Motorsport car, although fast, was very nervous on a bumpy track. *Gran Turismo 3*: A-Spec arrived in Summer 2001 for the PlayStation 2, with even better graphics and game play, along with the chance to drive Vauxhall's Elise-based VX220. There was even a special edition, *Gran Turismo Concept 2002 Tokyo-Geneva*, which featured the Heritage special edition Elise Type 72.

Other driving games which feature the enduring Elise include *Vanishing Point*, Acclaim Entertainment's attempt to tackle *Gran Turismo* and available for playing on the Sega Dreamcast and Sony PlayStation. Like the Sony game, *Vanishing Point* offers a tune-up shop to boost vehicle specifications, and there is the extra challenge of a 'Stunt Driver Challenge' mode in addition to standard arcade racing.

---

leak through the plastic intake manifold, or through fuses blowing on the electric fans prior to a period in heavy traffic. Thus, with any used car look out for the signs of a blown head gasket: be wary if there is mayonnaise-like goo in the oil filler cap, bubbles on the dipstick, oil in the coolant, or excessive white smoke from the exhaust. If you are concerned, get an expert in to check it out for peace of mind.

'If it's looked after properly it should go on forever,' said Bell & Colvill's road and race Elise specialist John Shorrocks, 'we've seen cars with up to 80,000 miles with little or no problems.' Proper looking after really means a full service history from a Lotus

main dealer. There is little excuse for avoiding it as servicing is far from crippling in performance car terms, as Bell noted: 'If you are realistic there are no nasty shocks with an Elise, there is nothing on the car that is hideously expensive'. Analyse the service history to make sure it has at least received its regular service every 12 months or 9,000 miles (6,000 miles for the Exige/340R/Sport 160) and the all-important cambelt swap every 54,000 miles (36,000 miles for the Exige/340R/Sport 160). Look for evidence of the recommended coolant changes every 24 months, and new brake and clutch fluid every 12 months. If the car is regularly punted around on track days, it should also

Lotus Challenge has a movie stuntman option in addition to the classic racing game to allow you to indulge in a passion for jumping school buses with an Exige. (Virgin Interactive)

The Gran Turismo *series offers excellent playability and relatively realistic handling on a wide range of Elises, from a standard car to the Sport Elise racer.* (Sony)

The Rover K-series engine should prove an economical and reliable companion, but look out for signs of a blown head gasket. (Tony Baker)

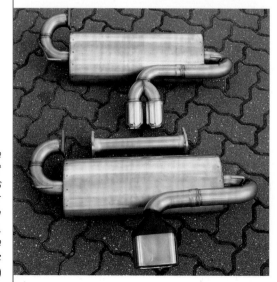

A popular and attractive option is an aftermarket stainless steel sports exhaust, which can offer more power and a much improved exhaust note, but may require the removal of the catalytic converter. (Bell & Colvill)

receive new oil every two or three outings in addition to its regular servicing. One problem the K-series does suffer is excessive carbon monoxide emissions that show up in an MoT test, but it should be possible to tune this out. In extreme cases, an abused and regularly and excessively over-revved engine will give up the ghost by cracking its cylinder liners, and it is worth bearing in mind that rebuilding any Elise motor is a £6,000 job. Standard exhaust tailpipes tend not to last particularly well, but if you spend the extra to buy a stainless steel system, as offered by numerous aftermarket companies in addition to Lotus itself, then not only will your Elise sound and breathe better, but the

Collectors' *lot*

For owners of enthusiasts' cars such as the Elise, collecting memorabilia and regalia related to the model can become almost an obsession – and for the Elise collector there is a lot out there.

If you're after an Elise to put on the shelf, quite a variety has become available since the car's launch. One of the first, in 1:43 scale, was the Vitesse die-cast S1, in standard, roll bar-equipped Sport 190 and Heritage 49 special edition trims. There was also a resin version from Provence Moulage, a white metal SMTS release and a more crude model, again of the standard Elise, from New Ray Co. Ltd. Other 1:43s include FFI's GT1 racer, and Lotus even offered a model of the Motorsport race transporter. Moving up a scale, Vitesse also produced a 1:18 Elise, Chrono offered an excellent die-cast GT1 and Maisto released an Opel Speedster in 2001. But if you prefer models to be more than just static displays, the 1:6 scale Schumacher Sport Elise kit was remote controlled, featured independent suspension and was capable of reaching its 55mph (88.5km/h) top speed in just two seconds.

Throughout the life of the Elise, Lotus recognised the power the little car had created as a brand. The Lotus Customer Experience Centre at Hethel was set up in 1999 as a showcase for a whole range of Lotus clothing and memorabilia, which was dominated by the Elise selection. The items were also available through Lotus Special Vehicle Options, from franchised dealers, and through both the Official Lotus Club and the independent Club Lotus. To show their affiliation, Elise owners and enthusiasts could wear T-shirts, sweatshirts, fleeces and pin badges, all sporting the now-classic Elise script, as featured on the tail of the car itself. There were also the usual branded goods you never knew you couldn't live without, such as a sports watch, cigarette lighter, key fob and clamshell screwdriver and Allen key sets.

With the Elise S2 came a whole new range featuring the new Elise branding of the Steven Crijns-penned silhouette and stylised script. By then the selection of Elise clothing had become more high-street fashion wear than bobble-hatted enthusiast fodder. There were shirts, fleeces and some smart jackets, as well as a new-style key fob and stylish sports watch and, recalling the Elise chassis, an extruded aluminium CD holder.

The more extreme Elise-based creations were not forgotten either, with a separate Exige range including jacket, fleece, shirt, baseball cap and key ring. Products created to mark the 340R, such as a mouse mat and T-shirt, boasted a dynamic graphic representation of the car itself together with the 340R script. From Lotus Motorsport came the Lotus Sport range, a collection including shirts, jackets, hats, umbrella, key ring, mug, mouse mat and even a pen and lighter, all finished in the race support team's black and yellow colours and featuring the Sport Elise silhouette.

But for the compulsive collector the more interesting finds are rarely items available commercially, but publicity material or corporate gifts, such as the special Elise carrier bags given away at motor shows to celebrate the model's launch, or the beautifully functional desk tidy formed from the elegant aluminium pedal box extrusion. Of the brochures and advertising collectibles, press packs, early brochures and motor show give-aways are likely to become desirable, particularly for stillborn subjects such as the M250 (see Chapter 9).

Far left: Products designed specifically for the 340R, such as mouse mats and T-shirts, used this special stylised graphic depicting the car and its logo. (Lotus)

Left: Lotus used the pedal extrusion to create desk tidies to give away as corporate gifts – a future collector's item no doubt. (Tony Baker)

A poorly adjusted or worn gearbox linkage can result in a sloppy gearchange or sticking in gear. (Author)

problem of mild steel rotting through is eliminated.

If the engine has been known to suffer the odd malady, at least the Rover-sourced five-speed transmission is a very reliable unit. Problems are confined to occasional weaknesses in the synchromesh, and a sloppy or poorly engaging lever, indicating that the cable-operated linkage is out of adjustment or worn, a relatively inexpensive fix. The clutch is almost unbelievably hardwearing, as John Shorrocks explained: 'They don't go through clutches, we've only had to do one through wear'. But what of Richard Rackham's pedal box? Beautiful and functional it may be, but not without its faults. The clutch pedals on early cars can

become sticky and seize, or cause the bronze bush in the throttle pedal to wear, calling for a tricky and lengthy repair. Two options are available: either keep the clutch pedal mechanism lubricated with WD40 or a similar lubricant, or retrofit the nylon bush with stainless steel pivot as fitted to cars built from mid-1999 onwards.

Suspension and brakes

Thanks to the very stiff set-up of the Elise, there is little compliance in the suspension and the extra pressure this exerts means components do wear more than in ordinary road cars. Fortunately, however, the bushes prone to wear, such as the rear toe-links, the ball joints and the shock

absorbers, are relatively easy parts to bolt on and are not fiercely expensive. On a test drive, listen out for clonking from beneath, which usually signals worn anti-roll bar mounts, and look out for the sloppy feel that comes from tired bushes and dampers. Don't be put off by cars that have seen a lot of track use and feel a bit loose though, as the Elise was built to take it and the chances are it will be transformed by rebushing and the fitting of a set of new shock absorbers. Another problem to affect early cars was prematurely worn wheel bearings, a trait that has since been solved. More worrying would be a car that tracks badly on the road or suffers from judder through the steering, as these can indicate suspension geometry put out of line by accident damage.

All Elise variants are impressively gentle on brakes, thanks to their light weight, but different criteria apply depending on the age of the car. The metal matrix composite (MMC) discs available for the first year and a half of production offer enormous pad life of 30-40,000 miles, and the discs themselves should last as long as the car. However, John Shorrocks warned against cars fitted with these dics which are regularly extended on track days: 'They don't like track use, they don't shed heat and can overheat, look out for scoring all round the disc where there should be a uniform blue/grey band.' Replacements are hard to find, costly and

Rear suspension balljoints and toe-link bushes are prone to wear and can promote wayward handling. Later cast-iron discs will not last as long as MMC ones, but they suffer less from track day use. (Author)

Take it to the max

If a standard Elise isn't quick enough, stiff enough or, at the other end of the scale, isn't comfortable enough, then there are two routes you can take for upgrades: either rom Lotus direct or from a range of specialist suppliers.

Although there are a huge number of modifications available to boost the power output, braking and handling of the Elise, Lotus evaluation engineer Alastair McQueen warned against some unapproved kits: 'From time to time we get the opportunity to drive modified Elises. Most have modified engines, but there were a couple with suspension modifications and they really screwed the car up, they took all the progression out of the handling.' The first port of call for most Elise owners looking to improve their cars tends to be Lotus itself. McQueen explained the K-series engine options available: 'We've got everything from the base engine at 118bhp for S1 and 120bhp for S2, with kits for 135, 145, 160 and 190bhp – and there's the 177bhp standard Exige and 340R engine.' Rather than buy a whole engine kit, you could also find a few extra bhp with a pipe that replaces the catalytic converter (for track use only), with a competition air filter or one of the in-house sports exhaust systems, which have the bonus of sounding that bit better too.

To cope with extra power, the Lotus Special Vehicle Options list, much of which was developed in conjunction with Lotus Motorsport, also included a variety of gearbox options, from the close-ratio item standardised for the S2, to units with straight-cut or dog-gear internals, and a limited slip differential. Although drilled and ventilated discs, four-pot calipers and uprated pads are available, McQueen reckoned that the standard set-up is good enough for most applications: 'Braking has never required any upgrading because the car is well braked for its weight, and even with the 190bhp cars we've never had any problems.'

For serious track day use, however, the standard Elise set-up is too soft and stiffer suspension is a must. Options included uprated Eibach springs and Koni dampers, a motorsport anti-roll bar, and a Uniball rear toe-link to better locate the tail and improve

stability. Using wider 6in front and 8in rear wheels improves grip, and Lotus worked with Yokohama to create its AO38 road-legal track tyres, which make a huge difference. 'There's a sport kit for the S1,' said McQueen, 'and we also have a Dynamics dampers option; they are very expensive but mean you can tweak the dampers on your own car.' But McQueen warned against altering the set-up of S2 cars without Lotus approval: 'The tyres on the Series 2 are unique to that car, you shouldn't fit non-Lotus tyres to your new Elise or it would seriously affect the handling.'

Outside of Lotus itself, numerous specialist suppliers and tuning firms have cashed in on the lucrative Elise upgrade market. Bell & Colvill produced a range of hotted-up Elise specials, the first being its 140bhp Elise Super 140 introduced at the Earls Court Motor Show in 1997. The Super 160 and 111S-based Sprint 170 followed, along with the turbocharged Super 180, 200 and 220. Power Train Projects (PTP), the people who developed the Sport 135 and VHPD engines, offered a range of engine tunes up to 220bhp, with a turbocharged unit reinforced with forged pistons, steel rods, bespoke cams, lightened flywheel and a VHPD-derived head. The unit was tractable, but didn't really come alive until the revs rose, with peak torque of 154lb ft (209Nm) arriving at 6,750rpm and that peak power some 1,500rpm later. It offered 150mph (241km/h), but at a price – over £10,000 fitted.

Not all upgrades need to be costly however. A simple chip, such as the 12bhp boost from the ABP Motorsport superchip, could be had for under £200, while performance filters, including the K&N offering, can also liberate a few bhp. Moto-build Racing offered good value performance upgrades, with its Stage II kit boosting the standard Elise to 150bhp and the Stage I kit for the 111S offering 157bhp. Quorn Engine Developments created an exciting option to its 200bhp engine conversion when it inserted a six-speed sequential gearbox, something that was also offered by Quaife. This unit was derived from the MG Rover rally car with a specialist casing and dog gear internals, and its snappy push/pull operation was an exciting, if expensive, track day option.

Quick to get in on the act of achieving the near impossible and improving on the stunning S2 was Turbo Technics, which

developed the TT190 engine upgrade. This option used a small, neat-fitting centrifugal supercharger to give lag-free power throughout the rev band, without the peaky nature of the VHPD unit. For around £6,000 you got 190bhp at 6,500rpm, 170lb ft (230Nm) at 5,000rpm and 0-60mph in 4.6 seconds, but Turbo Technics had more to offer. If an Exige was not enough, the supercharged TT260 Supersport boosted the VHPD unit to 270bhp and 207lb ft (281Nm) of torque giving loads of usable power at all engine speeds and 0-60mph in a shade over four seconds. Even more extreme was the 300bhp BBR turbo Elise, and there have also been moves to follow the Caterham Blackbird and Westfield Megabusa along the motorcycle engine route.

Various companies have tried their hands at improving the already exceptional Elise suspension, with kits offering stiffer springs and adjustable dampers with anti-roll bars available from, among others, QED, Pilbeam and Spyder Engineering. Attempts to improve braking have also been made, such as drilled and grooved discs, Aeroquip hosing or harder fast road and race pads such as EBC Greenstuff.

If you were after a bit more comfort, Lotus could kit your Elise out with removable mats or even a full carpet set. To personalise it there was the 111S-style rear wing on the options list, while for the interior there were smart aluminium window winders, heater knobs, handbrake sleeve and gear knob. The Exige had its own range of satin black trim options, but if your interest was more competition than cosmetics, Lotus could fit an Elise with Corbeau competition seats – or carbon-fibre race seats for the S2, with harnesses, a quick-release Momo steering wheel, roll cage and even a plumbed-in fire extinguisher.

Specialists were able to offer conversions to leather trim and leather-covered door panels, or tailor-made fitted luggage to capitalise on the Elise's limited boot space. For Continental touring, Lotus offered a luggage rack that fitted over the engine cover, offering ungainly looks but much improved capacity. While for the amateur racer, the Kelsport division of Kelvedon Lotus offered the usual engine, braking and suspension upgrades, and also developed its own roll cages, a fuel tank safety cell and lightweight panels including a new front clamshell with integral spoiler.

usually second-hand. The ventilated cast-iron discs on later cars, whether standard or drilled, as on the higher performance versions, will wear out pads from as little as 4,500 miles or as much as 30,000 miles. Wear usually depends on how much track use the car has had, although numerous fast road and race pad compounds are available. Discs usually last around three sets of pads, but if they are badly worn replacements are not excessively expensive.

Look out for the telltale signs of an unloved car, such as kerbed alloys or scratches and bashes in the composite bodywork. Stone chips around the nose and aft of each wheelarch are normal, but look for evidence of more serious accident damage, such as mismatched paint. Bobby Bell reckoned you should not be put off entirely by a car that has had a shunt, as long as only cosmetic work is required. 'It is not dramatically more expensive to

A selection of the parts, accessories and upgrades on offer from the wide variety of specialists catering for the Elise. (Bell & Colvill)

You can even customise the interior of your Elise, just don't add too much weight! (Bell & Colvill)

The higher state of tune of the VHPD engine means that it is less likely to last for high mileages without requiring a rebuild; the 190bhp version is particularly highly stressed. (Tony Baker)

repair than metal,' he explained, 'and the clamshells are not all that expensive, so if you crunch the glassfibre significantly then just replace the clams. If the chassis is not bent and you put new clamshells on then it's as good as new, much more so than a steel-bodied car. The process of fitting new clamshells is not remotely detrimental to the car's integrity.' Replacing clamshells and panels on S2 versions should be even cheaper thanks to the less labour-intensive construction method replacing the hand-lay of the more complicated S1. In addition to the glassfibre,

watch out for stonechips or cracks in the costly bonded-in headlamp cowls offered as optional extras or standard fit on more powerful versions. The grille-mounted spotlamps are also prone and replacements are expensive, so check their condition. Many owners have fitted guard film or covers to ensure they remain intact.

An advantage of the spartan Elise is that there is little inside the car that can go wrong, thanks particularly to the lack of complex electrics. In addition to the obligatory leaky roof, water can penetrate the cabin if the bonded-in sill trims have been damaged by careless entry and exit, with replacement a tricky job. Hoods are prone to tears, particularly on the complex S1 version, and to damaged fittings and clips through their fiddly and at times frustrating operation. On early cars, the felt window runners can distort and grab the window, which can pop the mechanism apart if it is forced. The fittings within the doors are bonded-in and once they come away there is no permanent fix, so check their operation and be wary of a stiff mechanism or dropped window glass.

One of the teething problems of early S2 cars was the dashboard covering bubbling up in summer heat, but the majority of afflicted cars will have had the problem remedied under warranty with new glue formulated to be less sensitive to temperature changes. A further problem to look out for on early S2s is bent keys and damage to the engine cover, due to the first cars requiring the cover to be lifted by the key, still turned in the lock. This can be improved by retrofitting the later spring release that pops the lid up enough to lift by hand.

The Exige, 340R and Sport 190 bring with them their own set of additional problems because of their spectacular state of tune and overt track intentions, mostly due to the Very High Performance Derivative (VHPD) K-series engine. 'You've got to be aware that it's a pretty highly tuned engine,' explained Bobby Bell. 'The intermediately tuned cars are OK, but when you have an engine that revs to 8,000rpm then everything is that bit more stressed, it's pretty much a race engine. I can't see them doing more than 40,000 miles before being stripped and rebuilt.' This is a view shared by John Shorrocks: 'It depends on use and care,' he said. 'We've seen cars that only do track days with no problems at all. If you were unlucky, it could be as little as 5,000 miles before needing a rebuild, but if you treat it right and use it properly there is

Look out for cracked headlamp cowls and excessive stone chipping around the nose. Exige front splitters are easily damaged by speed humps. (Tony Baker)

no reason why it shouldn't do 30–40,000.'

In addition to more regular servicing, oil level and condition are critical to the longevity of VHPD engines. Regular changes with good quality oil are required and a potential buyer should check it carefully. Listen out for rattling from the unit on the move and look out for blue smoke as signs of imminent failure, and if there is metallic deposit on the dipstick, walk away because that engine is a goner. Head gaskets are still on the checklist, but unusually the higher-tune unit runs cooler than the standard car so it should be less prone to blowing. An area where the Exige suffers in particular is damage to its super-low front splitter when being driven in town, where it will ground at every opportunity and the glassfibre can crack and splinter.

But whichever model you decide to go for, buy carefully and an Elise should prove to be a faithful and relatively inexpensive companion.

9 **Where to** now?

Lotus must be wondering if its designers and engineers have the Midas touch, certainly the Elise S1 and S2 are pure gold. But what's next? Will the Elise follow the lead of the first Elan, its illustrious predecessor, evolving into S3, S4, Sprint and four-seater +2? Or will it still be in production to celebrate its 30th birthday, like the restyled 2002 Esprit which, although somewhat archaic, retained the core appeal that made it such a great car at its 1972 launch? Will the S2 sire a hardtop Exige or radical 340R variant, or will Lotus continue down the comfort-orientated path it has struck with tourer packs and air-

conditioning? With cars such as Toyota's MR2 and the MGF offering sequential and steptronic transmissions, maybe it is time for Lotus to address the criticisms of the Elise gearbox and offer something a bit more innovative. Similarly, will the next Elise feature conventional power or the very fashionable option of a rev-hungry motorcycle unit? Gavan Kershaw was sceptical of the sequential option: 'It's been done. You can buy one, but for a stupid amount of money. In the right environment it's the best thing since sliced bread, but try to drive through a city centre, the amount of

Will there be a closed Exige version of the S2 Elise? . . . (Tony Baker)

times that you cruise up to a junction in fourth, dip the clutch and brake. All of a sudden you've got to bang down all these gears rather than just knock it into neutral and away you go again.'

One major plus for the future of the Elise is its fantastic chassis, which offers amazing flexibility as its designer Richard Rackham explained. 'As far as the tub is concerned, it's still got huge potential. You can easily drop different bodies on to it, things can be done to make it quieter and cooler in the summer, there's a long way to go.' Project manager Tony Shute sees a future for two Elises, a more comfortable car and an extreme one, possibly taking its inspiration from his own Exposé project: 'I'd like to see us develop the S2 to make it more into an Elan (M100) in some ways, and at the same time keep a radical direction on it as well. We mustn't forget the niche that it's aimed at. I love the chassis still, it's a great attribute for the car, I'd like to get some more models out of it.'

One thing is for sure, as long as there is an Elise there will be rivals to keep the engineers

at Lotus busy shifting the goalposts further forward. Alastair McQueen hoped Lotus would be able to maintain its high standards in the face of ever-tightening restrictions: 'The competition is never far behind and we have to put a lot of effort in to maintain that dynamic performance. I'm afraid it may well be legislated against us eventually and we won't be able to build cars like the Elise. I hope we can, it's a very pure car and there are so few new cars like that around, there's no corruption through power assistance, driver aids or technology for that matter.' As the BMW Z3 is replaced by the Z4 it promises more power and better handling, but also manages to become more of a polar opposite to Elise as it adds girth, weight and price. The new Mercedes-Benz SLK looks to be heading in a similar direction, but keenly-priced 200bhp versions of both the Mazda MX-5 and MGTF (the MGF replacement) could tempt Elise buyers simply with their straight-line speed.

Of more concern are the cars that have followed Elise: lightweight, high-performance sports cars in the Lotus mould. The British-

. . . or will there be an option of occasional rear seats as in the classic Lotus Elan +2? (LAT)

Competitors such as the Leading Edge 190RT will ensure that the Elise will have to keep upping its game to stay ahead of the field. (Olivier Gires)

built Vemac Car Co. RD180 is said to match Elise ride and handling, thanks to former Lotus man John Miles, and it certainly looks like the Hethel product. But its 173bhp Honda VTEC engine struggles with its 940kg (2,073lb) and a price tag of £44,000 keeps it

well out of Elise territory. The Tommy Kaira ZZ has been reborn as the 190RT from Norfolk-based Leading Edge and from Venturi, France's answer to Lotus, comes the attractive and exciting-sounding Fetish. The model is to feature aluminium and composite construction, a mass-produced motor and a £22,000 price tag – sound familiar? And then there are the super-light motorcycle-engined cars that many see as the future of the small sports car. The carbon-fibre monocoque Bebi Spider by Giotto Bizzarrini has a target weight of just 400kg (882lb) and a 1,300cc Suzuki Hayabusa bike engine would offer 175bhp. While the AS One from German firm Automotive Solutions boasts 452bhp/tonne thanks to an impressive 235bhp and 520kg (1,147lb).

At Geneva in March 2002, a Lotus Engineering concept dropped a huge hint at a possible future for Elise, a million miles from the frenetic high-revving bike-engined cars. Called Project ECO_2S (pronounced 'ECOS'), the familiar-looking car was designed as a low carbon emissions sports car, anticipating legislation restricting CO_2 emissions to 120–140g/km by 2010. Although the Elise is already pretty environmentally friendly, ECO_2S would offer paltry CO_2 emissions of under 75g/km and awesome economy of an average of 70mpg (4 litres/100km), yet still hit 62mph (100km/h) from rest in just 6.2 seconds and reach a maximum of 124mph (200km/h). Much like the Elise, the new car was designed to be based on a lightweight bonded and riveted aluminium chassis with composite crash structure and the metal matrix composite brake discs first seen on the Elise S1. ECO_2S would be slightly longer and wider – and hence heavier – than the Elise, with injection-formed thermoplastic composite body panels and multilink rear suspension replacing the Elise's double wishbones. The biggest difference however, would be the engine. For some time, Lotus Engineering's powertrain section had been concentrating on diesel technology, and at the time of the ECO_2S's unveiling it was developing its

own in-house diesel V8, but the new car would feature a bought-in unit as does the Elise. The 1.2-litre turbo diesel engine would use direct injection to improve fuel economy and reduce emissions, and feature a Lotus Engineering-developed electro-hydraulic active valve train (AVT) system. The AVT replaces the traditional camshaft and valve lifters with electrical actuators and four-valves per cylinder, employing active combustion to improve combustion stability and reduce fuel consumption and emissions. The innovations continued with a continuously variable transmission and a

nifty active noise control system to ensure the car would still sound like a sports car, despite its diesel engine.

But there is a school of thought that says the next Elise should not be quite so extreme, could be a bit bigger, a bit more comfortable. After talking to his customers, Bobby Bell of dealer Bell & Colvill plc suggested a car he would like to see. 'We should have a bigger Elise with a three-litre engine, a soft top and removable hardtop, that's easier to get in and out of, because that really does limit the market.' It looks like that may well be the way to go.

At the Geneva Motor Show in 2002, Lotus unveiled the ECO$_2$S, a diesel-powered Elise concept for model year 2010. It would retain the extruded aluminium chassis principles of the Elise, while offering even greater economy and lower emissions. (Lotus)

153

The next major step for the Elise is to cross the water and meet America, a market not ventured into since the front-drive Elan bombed over there at the turn of the 1990s. The firm had being laying the groundwork for the move, acquiring in 2001 a new testing and development facility business in Ann Arbor, Michigan, with Lotus Engineering opening a new engineering centre in nearby Southfield. Opinions differ as to whether the idea of sending the Elise to the USA is a good one. Chassis engineer Richard Rackham was excited by the prospect: 'I would love to see the car go to America if it can be made to work commercially. Elise 2 is a much higher quality vehicle than Elise 1, my personal view is that the car would go down very well there.' But friend and former colleague Julian Thomson was more sceptical. 'I can't really see it working to be

honest, I may be proved wrong. It's so difficult to actually market anything in America with a small budget, which worries me, but maybe they can do it; good luck to them. It's going to be tricky but then again America is a huge place so perhaps you don't need to find that big a percentage of customers.'

Long-time Lotus man Roger Becker was the engineer put in charge of creating the Federal Elise, codenamed M260. 'The question is continually asked: "Why didn't you put the first car into America?" and, "Why did you then make the second car and not put it into America either?" We were concerned that the quality level of the S1 would be inferior to American customer expectation,' explained Becker, 'and that the required investment to turn it into a compliant USA car was too big for the company to entertain at the time. We were

Will the Elise finally make it to the USA? And how will Americans react to such an uncompromising driver's car? (Tony Baker)

M250: The future becomes the past

With the success of Elise, the high-profile Lotus image brought a ready market for new models, and plans were announced in the Official Lotus Club's Summer 1999 magazine for a new baby supercar to slot in between the Elise and Esprit. It would follow the Elise's lead with an all-new chassis using bonded extruded aluminium technology and was tagged Emas (Malaysian for gold, a nod to Group Lotus owners Proton) by then-chief executive Chris Knight. Officially codenamed M250, and known internally as Project Monaco, the new car was to be a mid-engined two-seat coupé with a target price of £40-50,000, aiming it squarely at accomplished rivals such as the Porsche Boxter S. The car followed a similar concept, codenamed M230, which was also a cab-forward design using similar technology, but with two-plus-two accommodation.

The M250 was unveiled to an awestruck public in September 1999 at the Frankfurt Motor Show, and was developed further in time to star at October's London Motor Show at Earls Court. Although announced by Lotus as a concept car to gauge public reaction, it was obvious that the car had definite production potential and even Lotus Cars' own press releases demonstrated the intent. It stated: 'If it were to go into production [M250] would be in European dealerships during the first half of 2001, and be built in similar volumes to the Elise.' The M250's shape was not only stunning, taking inspiration from the 340R and giving a preview of the forthcoming Elise S2, but also revolutionary for its market sector. Wind tunnel testing and computer modelling helped designers develop a car with low drag and aerodynamic aids giving balanced downforce for high-speed stability, demonstrating lessons learned from the styling-led Elise. Careful design of the underbody to produce ground-effect also aided the car's stability with Lotus quoting a very conservative lift coefficient of −0.15.

But with innovation came style. Elegant doors lifted up and out, a combination of conventional, gullwing and Lamborghini-style 'scissor' doors, a solution that was both dynamic and practical, giving improved access to the cab-forward cockpit. The extruded aluminium chassis was to house a mid-mounted transverse dohc three-litre V6 developing 250bhp and running through a transverse six-speed gearbox to the rear wheels. To keep weight below a projected 1,000kg (2,200lb), the car would employ aluminium composite bodywork while composite floor and bulkheads would also give it 50 per cent more torsional stiffness than the Elise. The combination of power and light weight would take it from rest to 60mph in under five seconds, to 100mph in under 11 and on to a top speed electronically limited to 155mph (250km/h).

Despite being more about driver appeal than optional extras, M250's 2,518mm (99in) wheelbase allowed a roomy interior boasting leather and Alcantara trim, air conditioning, twin airbags and a useful luggage area behind the seats. For added refinement, soundproofing was to be integrated into the construction. Like the Elise, the M250 sported double wishbone suspension all round, but unlike its little brother the new car would offer power-assisted steering and ABS for its 320mm ventilated disc brakes. True to Lotus philosophy of driver appeal, traction and stability control would not feature, even on the options list.

Answering enthusiasts' prayers, Lotus decided to proceed and permitted its dealers to take deposits, the official order book opening at the beginning of 2000 for a projected launch in early 2002. The Official Lotus Club held a competition to give the car a traditional 'E' name and work on the M250 began in earnest, the first Lotus car to fully exploit the power of computer design and simulation techniques in its development. The M250 was intended to look pretty much as the concept that so many had fallen for, but there was confusion over which engine would be used. Units from Alfa Romeo and GM fitted the bill, but the concept car's engine was identified as Renault's Clio V6, an apparently logical choice as Renault had developed both conventional and sequential six-speed gearboxes. In

Autocar in June 2000, Renault executive vice president Pierre-Alain de Smedt confirmed the Renault V6 would be used, sparking rumours that the M250 might be used as a basis for a future Renault GTA. One car that would be based on the M250 chassis would be the parent company Proton's 'Ultimate' 2+2 coupé, due for launch at the 2003 Geneva show, and set to cost under £30,000 with a 200bhp two-litre 'four'.

Just as appetites were whetted for the new car, in January 2001 the project was delayed pending a global evaluation of its market potential. Lotus had decided that it needed a car to be sold worldwide and a feasibility study was set up to gauge its suitability for external markets and particularly the big one: USA. But it was merely a stay of execution. After a brief silence, and a further management reshuffle, incoming chief executive Terry Playle canned M250 in May 2001, announcing that it was to be replaced with a more luxurious supercar with worldwide appeal, to sell in far greater numbers than the projected 3,000 Europe-only M250s per year. Rather than lose the £30 million needed to put the car into production, it would be redesigned to cater for notoriously choosy US buyers, and notoriously rigorous US safety and emissions regulations. Bobby Bell of Lotus dealer Bell & Colvill voiced the dismay many felt at the loss: 'I was absolutely gutted, we had 170 orders, but the car was a little over-ambitious, those doors were asking for aggravation.' Lotus Cars sent letters out to well over 1,000 customers who had put down deposits to reserve cars, offering a refund of the £1,500 payment or a £3,000 discount on a new Elise or Esprit. Unfortunately, some buyers were left out of pocket as cash-strapped dealers closed, losing the additional payments held by the dealers themselves. As a further kick in the teeth, in late 2001 Lotus was forced to sell the Coventry research and design base where a team of up to 125 had undertaken much of the M250 development.

M250 was to cost Lotus dearly, both in pure financial terms and in customer loyalty. While its technology will almost certainly reappear in future Lotus models, enthusiasts of the Hethel marque will long mourn the abandonment of this super-stylish machine.

The wild M250 demonstration car shows what a spectacular machine the V6-powered coupé could have been. (Lotus)

A styling model shows the evolution from the Elise S1, S2 and Vauxhall VX220 to the stillborn Project M250. (Lotus)

Inside, the M250 carried on the Elise theme of exposed anodised aluminium surfaces, but with a bit more space and a lot more luxury. (Lotus)

Russell Carr's design for the M250 looks dynamic from any angle. (Lotus)

Most Elise fans will hope to see the model celebrate its 30th birthday, as the Esprit did in 2002. (Lotus)

than outshine the competition. In 'fully loaded' form it would cost $38,500, pitching it against the slower Audi TT 1.8 roadster and BMW Z3 3.0. More expensive than the Mazda MX-5, Toyota MR2 and Honda S2000, the US Elise would however significantly undercut the Mercedes SLK230, Porsche Boxster and home-grown Corvette. Not that Becker sees American cars as a threat: 'The only cars that will perform to the level that this car will perform are really big V8-engined cars: Corvettes, Camaros, Mustangs.' During the show, the Lotus team handed out questionnaires to visitors to gauge their reaction to the car, and of 500 surveys some 173 were considered serious prospects. The team also videotaped some of the visitors' reactions, such as:

'I thought it'd be three times that much.'

'It's totally different to anything I've seen before. It's a beautiful car.'

'Keep it simple, keep it lightweight and bring it to us.'

'It's just like what a perfect sports car should be.'

Or the ultra-American: 'Dad, I need this car.'

For those that fear the whole character of the Elise will be destroyed by the addition of all the niceties the American market demands, Becker's news is both good and bad. 'We don't want to destroy the lightweight principle of the Elise,' he explained, 'and we don't take on the likes of the Z3, TT or S2000 on feature because feature means weight, that's not what Lotus is about. But you do have to think about offering the Elise with feature levels the purist would spit at; the USA car will automatically have air-con as standard.' Becker denied that the suspension will be softened slightly to suit local tastes and rural roads, but there may be ABS and certainly airbags. The biggest change will be the loss of the venerable K-series engine. 'The Rover powertrain is not "federalisable" as the engine is not capable of meeting the stringent Federal emissions durability requirements,' Becker explained. Press suggestions that the Speedster's GM

not absolutely convinced of the numbers and many people still remembered the sad demise of the Elan 2 in the USA, but we have now thoroughly researched the market in terms of Elise product positioning and performance expectation. We've examined this market more than any other, because you have to get it right, it's such a technical and financial undertaking; go there and you can't afford to fail.' But succeed and even a tiny portion of the market should yield 1,500-2,000 extra sales, boosting production to around 5,000 cars per annum, requiring an expansion of existing dealer network, which at the turn of the millennium had only to deal with annual sales of around 150 Esprits.

Becker and his team tested the water for a potential USA Elise in January 2002 by taking the Series 2 car to the Greater Los Angeles Auto Show for its first Stateside appearance. Although the final specifications were not revealed, the public were told it would boast a new Federally compliant powertrain that would give the slightly heavier car a performance that would more

engine might be employed were soon replaced with speculation that the new unit would come from a Japanese source, with Toyota looking favourite over Honda's VTEC. But Lotus would not confirm or deny, only reiterate that the car would have very good performance despite the weight added by an improved specification and the beefed up chassis, crash structure and side-impact protection to get through tough US crash regulations. It could also mean a stripped out version would be the highest-performing Elise yet; move over 340R.

Whatever the future holds for this revolutionary sports car, the Elise's place in history is secure. A classic from the day it hit the road, the little Lotus has moved from the cover of modern car magazines to the cover of classic car magazines. In 2002, *Classic & Sports Car* ran the cover line: 'Is this the best ever Lotus?' But to many it is the best small sports car of all time, proving that in an age where electronics rule and bigger is better, where we are cosseted and insulated from the world outside, there is still room for a machine that focuses on the pure thrill of driving.

The Elise has come a long way since the first road car was released to the press. The next giant leap for the little Lotus success story will be tackling America. (LAT)

Appendix 1

Model specifications and performance figures

Reproduced with kind permission of *Autocar*
* Manufacturers' figures
\# Figures for 190bhp engine option

Lotus Elise 1.8i. (Tony Baker)

1996 Lotus Elise 1.8i
New price   £18,950

Dimensions:
Length	3,726mm (146.7in)
Width	1,820mm (71.7in)
Height	1,202mm (47.3in)
Wheelbase	2,300mm (90.6in)
Front track	1,440mm (56.7in)
Rear track	1,453mm (57.2in)
Kerb weight	723kg (1,594lb)
Weight distribution (f:r)	39:61
Turning circle	10.0m (32ft 9in)

Engine:
Type   MEMS fuel-injected all-alloy
                    4-cylinder in-line, 1,796cc,
                    16v dohc

Bore/stroke	80.0/89.3mm
Location	transverse, mid, rear-wheel drive
Max power	118bhp @ 5,500rpm
Max torque	122lb ft (165Nm) @ 3,000rpm
Bhp/tonne	163

Mechanics:
Transmission	five-speed manual transaxle
Suspension	*front:* double wishbones, coil springs over monotube dampers, anti-roll bar
	rear: double wishbones, coil springs over monotube dampers
Brakes	hydraulic, 282mm ventilated aluminium discs
Steering	rack and pinion, 2.7 turns lock to lock
Tyres	185/55 VR15 (F), 205/50 VR16 (R)

Performance:
0–60mph	5.5sec
0–100mph	17.4sec
60–0mph	3.0sec
Standing ¼ mile	14.3sec/93mph (150km/h)
30–50mph in 4th	5.0sec
50–70mph in 4th	5.1sec
30–70mph through gears	5.8sec
Max speed	124mph (200km/h)
Average consumption	28.7mpg (9.9 litres/100km)

1997 Lotus Elise Sport 190
As 1996 Lotus Elise 1.8i except:
New price £33,500

Dimensions:
Kerb weight	673kg (1,484lb)
Weight distribution (f:r)	n/a

Engine:
Max power	190bhp @ 7,500rpm
Max torque	150lb ft (203Nm) @ 5,750rpm
Bhp/tonne	283

Mechanics:
Suspension	*front:* double wishbones, coil springs over Koni competition monotube dampers, adjustable anti-roll bar, adjustable spring platforms
	rear: double wishbones, coil springs over Koni competition monotube dampers, adjustable anti-roll bar, adjustable spring platforms
Brakes	hydraulic, 282mm cross-drilled and ventilated cast-iron discs
Tyres	185/55 ZR15 (F), 225/45 ZR16(R)

Performance:
0–60mph	4.4sec
0–100mph	10.7sec*
60–0mph	n/a
Standing ¼ mile	n/a
30–50mph in 4th	n/a
50–70mph in 4th	n/a
30–70mph through gears	n/a
Max speed	141mph (227km/h)
Average consumption	n/a

Lotus Elise Sport 190. (LAT)

Lotus Elise GT1. (LAT)

1997 Lotus GT1*
As 1996 Lotus Elise 1.8i except:
New price   n/a

Dimensions:
Length	4,495mm (177in)
Width	2,070mm (81.5in)
Height	1,100mm (43.3in)
Wheelbase	2,675mm (105.3in)
Front track	1,700mm (66.9in)
Rear track	1,643mm (64.7in)
Kerb weight	900kg (1,984.5lb)
Weight distribution (f:r)	n/a
Turning circle	n/a

Engine:
Type	competition fuel injected 32v V8, 3,506cc, with two Allied Signal intercooled turbochargers and Lotus Racing EFI engine management (or 6.0-litre Corvette LT5 V8)
Bore/stroke	83/81mm
Location	longitudinal, mid, rear-wheel drive
Max power (road/race)	350bhp/550bhp
Max torque	n/a
Bhp/tonne (road/race)	389/611

Mechanics:
Transmission	Hewland six-speed manual
Suspension	*front:* solid, rose-jointed pickups with upper rocker arm and lower wishbone, racing coil springs over lightweight dampers
	rear: solid, rose-jointed pickups with upper rocker arm and lower wishbone, racing coil springs over lightweight dampers
Brakes	hydraulic, 355mm ventilated cast-iron or carbon discs with AP Racing aluminium six-pot calipers
Steering	n/a
Tyres	Michelin Pilot MXX3 295 ZR18 (F), 365 ZR18 (R)

Performance: n/a

1998 Lotus Elise Sport 135

As 1996 Lotus Elise 1.8i except:
New price   £28,950

Dimensions:

Kerb weight	740kg (1,632lb)
Weight distribution (f:r)	40:60
Turning circle	10.0m (32ft 9in)

Engine:

Max power	135bhp @ 6,500rpm
Max torque	130lb ft (176Nm) @ 5,000rpm
Bhp/tonne	182

Mechanics:

Transmission	close ratio five-speed manual transaxle
Brakes	hydraulic, 282mm ventilated cast-iron drilled discs
Steering	rack and pinion, 2.7 turns lock to lock
Tyres	185/55 VR15 (F), 205/45 VR16 (R)

Performance:

0–60mph	5.8sec
0–100mph	17.7sec
60–0mph	2.8sec
Standing ¼ mile	14.7sec/94mph (151km/h)
30–50mph in 4th	5.3sec
50–70mph in 4th	5.3sec
30–70mph through gears	6.1sec
Max speed	127mph (204km/h)
Average consumption	27.7mpg (10.2 litres/100km)

Lotus Elise Sport 135.
(LAT)

1999 Lotus Elise 111S

As 1996 Lotus Elise 1.8i except:
New price   £26,590

Dimensions:

Kerb weight	770kg (1,698lb)

Engine:

Type	all-alloy 4-cylinder in-line, 1,796cc, 16v dohc with variable valve timing and MEMS multi-point sequential fuel injection
Max power	143bhp @ 7,000rpm
Max torque	128lb ft (174Nm) @ 4,500rpm
Bhp/tonne	186

Mechanics:

Transmission	close ratio five-speed manual transaxle
Brakes	hydraulic, 282mm ventilated cast-iron drilled discs
Tyres	185/55 ZR15 (F), 225/45 ZR16 (R)

Performance:

0–60mph	5.6sec
0–100mph	11.7sec
60–0mph	2.9sec
Standing ¼ mile	14.2sec/99mph (159km/h)
30–50mph in 4th	5.3sec
50–70mph in 4th	5.4sec
30–70mph through gears	5.2sec
Max speed	130mph (209km/h)
Average consumption	30.7mpg (9.2 litres/100km)

Lotus Elise 111S.
(Lotus)

Lotus Sport Elise.
(Author)

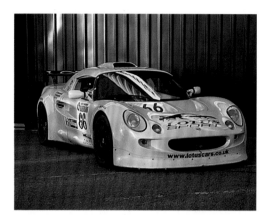

1999 Lotus Sport Elise*

As 1996 Lotus Elise 1.8i except:
New price £55,000 (for a season of racing)

Dimensions:
Kerb weight   700kg (1,544lb)
Weight distribution (f:r)   n/a
Turning circle   n/a

Engine:
Type   fuel injected all-alloy 4-cylinder
                                     in-line, 1,796cc, 16v dohc with
multi-point injection and Lotus
engine management
Max power   203bhp
Max torque   150lb ft (203Nm)
Bhp/tonne   290

Mechanics:
Transmission   Quaife straight-cut five-speed
                                     manual
Suspension   *front:* double wishbones, Eibach
                                     coil springs over two-way adjust-
                                     able dampers, adjustable anti-roll
                                     bar
                                     rear: double wishbones, Eibach
                                     coil springs over two-way
                                     adjustable dampers
Brakes   hydraulic, 295mm cross-drilled
                                     and ventilated cast-iron discs
                                     with four-piston front and two-
                                     piston rear calipers
Tyres   190/58 R16 (F), 230/62.5 R17
                                     (R)

Performance:
0–60mph   4.4sec
0–100mph   10.7sec
Remainder   n/a

164

1999 Lotus 340R
As 1996 Lotus Elise 1.8i except:
New price £35,000

Dimensions:
Length	3,620mm (142.5in)
Width	1,655mm (65.2in)
Height	1,123mm (44.2in)
Front track	1,432mm (56.4in)
Rear track	1,459mm (57.4in)
Kerb weight	675kg (1,488lb)
Weight distribution (f:r)	37:63

Engine:
Type	fuel injected all-alloy

4-cylinder in-line, 1,796cc, 16v dohc with multi-point injection and Lotus engine management

Max power	177bhp @ 7,800rpm
Max torque	126lb ft (171Nm) @ 5,000rpm
Bhp/tonne	262

Mechanics:
Transmission	close ratio five-speed manual transaxle
Brakes	hydraulic, ventilated and cross-drilled discs, 282mm front, 245mm rear
Tyres	195/50 ZR15 (F), 225/45 ZR16 (R)

Performance:
0–60mph	4.6sec
0–100mph	12.5sec
60–0mph	2.7sec
Standing ¼ mile	13.7sec/106mph (170.5km/h)
30–50mph in 4th	5.3sec
50–70mph in 4th	4.6sec
30–70mph through gears	4.2sec
Max speed	132mph (212km/h)
Average consumption	25.8mpg (11 litres/100km)

Lotus 340R. (Lotus)

2000 Lotus Elise Sport 160
As 1996 Lotus Elise 1.8i except:
New price n/a

Dimensions:
Kerb weight	770kg (1,698lb)

Weight distribution (f:r)	n/a

Engine:
Max power	160bhp @ 7,000rpm
Max torque	128lb ft (174Nm) @ 5,000rpm
Bhp/tonne	208

Mechanics:
Transmission	close ratio five-speed manual transaxle
Brakes	hydraulic, 282mm ventilated cast iron drilled discs
Tyres	185/55 ZR15 (F), 225/45 ZR16 (R)

Performance:
0-60mph	5.0sec
Remainder	n/a
Max speed	129mph (208km/h)
Average consumption	n/a

Lotus Elise Sport 160. (Dan Enticknap)

Lotus Exige. (Author)

2000 Lotus Exige

As 1996 Lotus Elise 1.8i except:
New price £29,995

Dimensions:

Length	3,780mm (148.8in)
Width	1,720mm (67.7in) (excl mirrors)
Height	1,175mm (46.3in)
Front track	1,440mm (56.7in)
Rear track	1,453mm (57.2in)
Kerb weight	785kg (1,731lb)
Weight distribution (f:r)	n/a
Turning circle	n/a

Engine:

Type	fuel injected all-alloy 4-cylinder

in-line, 1,796cc, 16v dohc with multi-point injection and Lotus engine management

Max power	177bhp @ 7,800rpm (190bhp @ 7,800rpm)
Max torque	127lb ft (172Nm) @ 6,750rpm (126lb ft (171Nm) @ 5,000rpm)
Bhp/tonne	242

Mechanics:

Transmission	close ratio five-speed manual transaxle
Brakes	hydraulic, ventilated and cross-drilled 282mm discs
Steering	rack and pinion, 2.3 turns lock to lock
Tyres	195/50 ZR16 (F), 225/45 ZR17 (R)

Performance:

0–60mph	5.4sec
0–100mph	13.7sec
60–0mph	2.7sec
Standing ¼ mile	14.0sec/101mph (162.5km/h)
30–50mph in 4th	7.9sec
50v70mph in top	10.1sec
30–70mph through gears	5.0sec
Consumption, worst/best	18.8-27.1mpg (15–10.4 litres/100km)

2000 Vauxhall VX220/Opel Speedster

As 1996 Lotus Elise 1.8i except
New price £22,995

Dimensions:

Length	3,790mm (149.2in)
Width	1,880mm (74in)
Height	1,112mm (43.8in)
Wheelbase	2,330mm (91.7in)
Front track	1,450mm (57in)
Rear track	1,494mm (58.8in)
Kerb weight	875kg (1,929lb)
Weight distribution (f:r)	n/a
Turning circle	11.25m (36ft 11in)

Engine:

Type	all-alloy 4-cylinder in-line, 2,198cc, 16v dohc with Bosch sequential fuel injection
Bore/stroke	80.0/89.3mm
Max power	145bhp @ 5,800rpm
Max torque	150lb ft (203Nm) @ 4,000rpm
Bhp/tonne	166

Mechanics:

Suspension	*front:* unequal length wishbones, coil springs, anti-roll bar *rear:* unequal length wishbones, coil springs
Brakes	hydraulic, servo-assisted 288mm ventilated discs with ABS
Steering	rack and pinion, 2.8 turns lock to lock
Tyres	175/55 R17 (F), 225/45 R17 (R)

Performance:

0–60mph	6.1sec
0–100mph	17.0sec
Standing ¼ mile	14.8sec/93mph (150km/h)
30–50mph in 4th	6.1sec
50–70mph in 4th	6.5sec
30–70mph through gears	6.4sec
Max speed	132mph (212km/h)
Average consumption	25.5mpg (1 litres/100km)

Vauxhall VX220. (Vauxhall)

Lotus Elise S2 1.8i.
(Lotus)

2001 Lotus Elise S2 1.8i
New price   £22,995

Dimensions:
Length	3,785mm (149in)
Width	1,880mm (74in)
Height	1,143mm (45in)
Wheelbase	2,300mm (90.5in)
Front track	1,457mm (57.4in)
Rear track	1,507mm (59.3in)
Kerb weight	750kg (1,654lb)
Weight distribution (f:r)	38:62
Turning circle	10.0m (32ft 9in)

Engine:
Type	MEMS fuel injected all-alloy 4-cylinder in-line, 1,796cc, 16v dohc
Bore/stroke	80.0/89.3mm
Location	transverse, mid, rear-wheel drive
Max power	120bhp @ 5,500rpm
Max torque	124lb ft (168Nm) @ 3,500–4,500rpm
Bhp/tonne	160

Mechanics:
Transmission	close ratio five-speed manual transaxle
Suspension	*front:* double wishbones, coil springs over Bilstein monotube dampers, anti-roll bar *rear:* double wishbones, coil springs over Bilstein monotube dampers
Brakes	hydraulic, 282mm ventilated cast iron discs
Steering	rack and pinion, 2.8 turns lock to lock
Tyres	175/55 VR16 (F), 225/45 VR17 (R)

Performance:
0–60mph	5.8sec
0–100mph	17.6sec
60–0mph	2.6sec
Standing ¼ mile	14.6sec/93mph (150km/h)
30–50mph in 4th	5.3sec
50–70mph in 4th	5.3sec
30–70mph through gears	5.7sec
Max speed	124mph (199.5km/h)
Average consumption	27.6mpg (10.3 litres/100km)

Lotus Elise S2 Sport 135.
(Lotus)

2001 Lotus Elise S2 Sport 135 *

As 2001 Lotus Elise S2 1.8i except:
New price   £24,730

Engine:
Max power	135bhp @ 5,750rpm
Max torque	129lb ft (175Nm) @ 5,200rpm
Bhp/tonne	180

Performance:
0–62mph	5.4sec
0–100mph	14.9sec
Remainder	n/a
Max speed	129mph (208km/h)
Average consumption	n/a

2002 Lotus Elise S2 Sport 190 *

As 2001 Lotus Elise S2 1.8i except:
New price £33,582

Dimensions:

Height	n/a
Kerb weight	710kg (1,566lb)
Weight distribution (f:r)	n/a

Engine:

Max power	190bhp @ 7,800rpm
Max torque	128lb ft (174Nm) @ 5,000rpm
Bhp/tonne	268

Mechanics:

Suspension	*front:* double wishbones, coil springs over two-way adjustable dampers, anti-roll bar
	rear: double wishbones, coil springs over two-way adjustable dampers
Brakes	hydraulic, 282mm ventilated, drilled cast iron discs with race pads
Tyres	Yokohama A048

Performance:

0–60mph	4.4sec
Remainder	n/a
Max speed	135mph (217km/h)
Average consumption	n/a

Lotus Elise S2 Sport 190. (Lotus)

2002 Lotus Elise S2 111S

As 2001 Lotus Elise S2 1.8i except:
New price £27,995

Dimensions:

Rear track	1,503mm (59.2in

Kerb weight	780kg (1,720lb)
Weight distribution (f:r)	n/a

Engine:

Max power	156bhp @ 7,000rpm
Max torque	129lb ft (175Nm) @ 4,650rpm
Bhp/tonne	200

Performance:

0–60mph	5.0sec
0–100mph	14.5sec
Standing ¼ mile	14.2sec/100mph (161km/h)
30–50mph in 4th	5.2sec
50–70mph in 4th	5.2sec
30–70mph through gears	5.2sec
Max speed	127mph (204km/h)
Average consumption	29.2mpg (9.7 litres/100km)

Lotus Elise S2 111S. (Lotus)

Appendix 2

Elise production figures

Model	1996	1997	1998	1999	2000	2001	2002#	Total#
Elise*	432	1,955	3,031	2,030	1,148	17	0	8,613
Elise CKD**	0	180	0	0	0	0	0	180
GT1	0	8	0	0	0	0	0	8
111S	0	0	2	1,150	335	2	0	1,489
Sport 160	0	0	0	0	312	25	0	337
340R	0	0	0	0	340	0	0	340
Exige	0	0	0	0	499	84	0	583
Elise S2*	0	0	0	0	5	1,856	1,189	3,050
S2 111/111S	0	0	0	0	0	0	146	146
Totals	432	2,143	3,033	3,180	2,639	1,984	1,335	14,746

*   Includes Sport 135 and Sport 190 performance kits
**   'Completely Knocked Down' kits supplied to Proton for assembly abroad
\#   To end of July 2002

Appendix 3

UK clubs and specialists

The following addresses, telephone numbers and internet details were believed correct at the time of going to press. However, as these are subject to change, no guarantee can be given for their continued accuracy.

Clubs

Club Lotus (and Team Elise)
41 Norwich Street
Dereham
Norfolk
NR19 1AD
Tel: 01362 694459/691144
Fax: 01362 695522
e-mail: clubhq@paston.co.uk

Lotus Drivers' Club
PO Box 9292
Alcester
Warwickshire
B50 4LD
www.lotusdriversclub.org

The Official Lotus Club
Lotus Cars
Hethel
Potash Lane
Norwich
NR14 8EZ
Tel: 0870 036 2277
Fax: 01953 608300
e-mail: olc@lotuscars.co.uk

750 Motor Club (Racing)
Lewes Enterprise Centre
112 Malling Street
Lewes
East Sussex
BN7 2RJ
Tel: 01825 750760
Fax: 01273 488750
www.motorsnippets.com/750mc

Aston Martin Owners' Club (Racing)
Drayton St Leonard
Wallingford
Oxfordshire
OX10 7BG
Tel: 01865 400400
Fax: 01865 400200
www.amoc.org

Lotus-approved UK dealers

Agnew Lotus
19 Boucher Crescent
Belfast
Northern Ireland
BT12 6HU
Tel:02890 686006
Fax:02890 686061

Bell & Colvill (Horsley) Ltd
Epsom Road
West Horsley
Nr Leatherhead
Surrey
KT24 6DG
Tel: 01483 281000
Fax: 01483 281999

Christopher Neil Ltd
Manchester Road
Northwick
Cheshire
CW9 7NA
Tel: 01606 41481
Fax: 01606 41642

CD Bramall
60 Northgate Street
Leicester
LE3 5BY
Tel: 01162 539700
Fax: 01162 14216

Dick Lovett (Cheltenham) Ltd
301 Gloucester Road
Cheltenham
Gloucestershire
GL51 7AP
Tel: 01242 253666
Fax: 01242 690612

Formula One
Albert Street
Newcastle upon Tyne
NE2 1YW
Tel: 0191 261 0383
Fax: 0191 221 1399

Freelance Motors (Guernsey) Ltd
Vale Garage Complex
Braye Road
Vale
Guernsey
GY3 5PA
Tel: 01481 242190
Fax: 01481 242136

Frosts Cars Ltd
394-398 Brighton Road
Shoreham-by-Sea
West Sussex
BN43 6RT
Tel: 01273 441400
Fax: 01273 440218

Gordon Lamb Ltd
1 Pomona Street
Sheffield
S11 8JH
Tel: 0114 262 5000
Fax: 0114 262 5010

H. R. Owen
125-133 Old Brompton Road
South Kensington
London
SW7 3RP
Tel: 0207 341 6300
Fax: 0207 341 6303

JCT 600 Brooklands
Ring Road
Lower Wortley
Leeds
LS12 6AA
Tel: 0113 389 0600   Fax: 0113 389 0610

H. R. Owen
318 Watford Road
Chiswell Green
St Albans
Hertfordshire
AL2 3DP
Tel: 01727 866171
Fax: 01727 811680

Motorway Sports Cars Ltd
Howfield Lane
Chartham
Canterbury
Kent
CT4 7HG
Tel: 01227 732233
Fax: 01227 732244

Murray Motor Co. Ltd
Bankhead Drive
Sighthill
Edinburgh
EH11 4DJ
Tel: 0131 442 2800
Fax: 0131 458 3296

Nick Whale Sports Cars Ltd
206 Bradford Street
Digbeth
Birmingham
B12 0RG
Tel: 0121 772 4250
Fax: 0121 772 4340

Orchard Dealerships
The Causeway
Great Billing
Northampton
NN3 9EX
Tel: 01604 403040
Fax: 01604 408698

Peter Smith Sports Cars Ltd
Station Road
Hatton
Derbyshire
DE6 5EL
Tel: 01283 813593
Fax: 01283 815491

Ribble Valley Lotus
Harwood Road
Rishton
Blackburn
Lancashire
BB1 4DJ
Tel: 01254 876876
Fax: 01254 883880

St Helier Garages Ltd
Unit 2
Rue Des Pres Trading Estate
St Saviour
Jersey
JE2 7QN
Tel: 01534 635555
Fax: 01534 635506

SGT Ltd
Station Road
Taplow
Maidenhead
Berkshire
SL6 0NT
Tel: 01628 605353
Fax: 01628 663467

Stratton Motor Company
Ipswich Road
Long Stratton
Norwich
Norfolk NR15 2XJ
Tel: 01508 530491
Fax:01508 531670

Westover Sports Cars Ltd
Salisbury Road
Pimperne
Blandford
Dorset
DT11 8UB
Tel: 01258 451211
Fax: 01258 451143

White Dove Garages
Hadfield Road
Cardiff
CF11 8WD
Tel: 02920 642999
Fax: 02920 344227

Williams Automobiles Ltd
St Philip's Causeway
Avon Meads
Bristol
BS4 4BD
Tel: 0117 3115000
Fax: 01179 728001

Wilson Lotus
145 High Road
Chadwell Heath
Romford
RM6 4AT
Tel: 0208 598 4120
Fax: 0208 597 9334

Index